MW00445816

WAR AGAINST THE JEWS

Also by Alan Dershowitz

Get Trump
Dershowitz on Killing
The Price of Principle
The Case for Vaccine Mandates
The Case for Color-Blind Equality in an Age of Identity Politics
The Case Against the New Censorship: Protecting Free Speech from Big Tech, Progressives, and
    Universities
Cancel Culture: The Latest Attack on Free Speech and Due Process
The Case for Liberalism in an Age of Extremism: or, Why I Left the Left But Can't Join the Right
Confirming Justice—Or Injustice?: A Guide to Judging RGB's Successor
Defending the Constitution
Guilt by Accusation: The Challenge of Proving Innocence in the Age of #MeToo
Defending Israel: The Story of My Relationship with My Most Challenging Client
The Case Against Impeaching Trump
The Case Against BDS: Why Singling Out Israel for Boycott Is Anti-Semitic and Anti-Peace
Trumped Up: How Criminalization of Political Differences Endangers Democracy
Electile Dysfunction: A Guide for Unaroused Voters
The Case Against the Iran Deal
Terror Tunnels: The Case for Israel's Just War Against Hamas
Abraham: The World's First (But Certainly Not Last) Jewish Lawyer
Taking the Stand: My Life in the Law
The Trials of Zion
The Case for Moral Clarity: Israel, Hamas and Gaza
The Case Against Israel's Enemies: Exposing Jimmy Carter and Others Who Stand in the Way of Peace
Is There a Right to Remain Silent? Coercive Interrogation and the Fifth Amendment After 9/11
Finding Jefferson: A Lost Letter, a Remarkable Discovery, and the First Amendment in the Age of
    Terrorism
Blasphemy: How the Religious Right is Hijacking Our Declaration of Independence
Pre-emption: A Knife That Cuts Both Ways
Rights From Wrongs: A Secular Theory of the Origins of Rights
America on Trial: Inside the Legal Battles That Transformed Our Nation
The Case for Peace: How the Arab-Israeli Conflict Can Be Resolved
The Case for Israel
America Declares Independence
Why Terrorism Works: Understanding the Threat, Responding to the Challenge
Shouting Fire: Civil Liberties in a Turbulent Age
Letters to a Young Lawyer
Supreme Injustice: How the High Court Hijacked Election 2000
Genesis of Justice: Ten Stories of Biblical Injustice that Led to the Ten Commandments and Modern Law
Just Revenge
Sexual McCarthyism: Clinton, Starr, and the Emerging Constitutional Crisis
The Vanishing American Jew: In Search of Jewish Identity for the Next Century
Reasonable Doubts: The Criminal Justice System and the O.J. Simpson Case
The Abuse Excuse: And Other Cop-Outs, Sob Stories, and Evasions of Responsibility
The Advocate's Devil
Contrary to Popular Opinion
Chutzpah
Taking Liberties: A Decade of Hard Cases, Bad Laws, and Bum Raps
Reversal of Fortune: Inside the Von Bülow Case
The Best Defense
Fair and Certain Punishment: Report of the 20th Century Fund Task Force on Criminal Sentencing
Courts of Terror: Soviet Criminal Justice and Jewish Emigration (coauthored with Telford Taylor)
Criminal Law: Theory and Process (with Joseph Goldstein and Richard Schwartz)
Psychoanalysis, Psychiatry, and Law (with Joseph Goldstein and Jay Katz)

WAR AGAINST THE JEWS

HOW TO END HAMAS BARBARISM

ALAN DERSHOWITZ

Hot Books

DEDICATION

War Against the Jews is dedicated to the brave soldiers of the Israeli Defense Forces who risk their lives to protect both Israeli and Palestinian civilians.

ACKNOWLEDGMENTS

This book could not have been completed so quickly without the assistance of Maura Kelly and Annie Hoyos, as well as the encouragement of Carolyn Cohen, Elon Dershowitz, and Alan Rothfeld.

Contents

Appendices

Introduction to Chapter 1

The murderous attack on Israeli civilians on October 7, 2023, and the responses to it, have changed everything. Israel's efforts to prevent its destruction by its deterrent strength has been weakened. This has encouraged Israel's enemies to redouble their efforts to commit politicide and genocide—to destroy the state of Israel and kill its citizens.

It has exposed rampant anti-Semitism around the world—especially among university students—even before Israel responded to the Hamas barbarity.

It has changed the relationship between Israel and the United States, especially with regard to American pressure on Israel and the possibility of direct American intervention.

It has required Israel to consider its nuclear options with regard to destroying Iran's nuclear weapons program and to deploying its nuclear arsenal as a last resort to assure its survival.

It has revealed dangerous attitudes among America's future leaders on today's college campuses toward Israel's possible destruction.

It has exposed media biases that have been exacerbated with Israel's vulnerabilities.

It has united most Israelis and Jews around the world as never before, despite the deep divisions among them politically, religiously, and ideologically.

It has also united many Arabs and Muslims both in America and througout the world around the Palestinian cause, despite their deep divisions.

It has shown that anti-Semitism increases when Jews and their nation state are victimized.

It has clouded the future of peace between Israel and its Arab and Muslim neighbors and has diminished the proposals for a peaceful resolution of the Israeli-Palestinian conflict.

It has made predictions about the future of the region nearly impossible, except that increasing instability is inevitable.

Nothing will ever be the same. It is remarkable that a ragtag band of murderous terrorists, conducting the largest pogrom against Jews since the Holocaust, could change so much in so little time.

There will be occasions in the future to assess how this perfect storm of Israeli vulnerability could have occurred. But for now, the focus must be on Israel's survival, and the steps it must take to restore its deterrents, to save as many hostages as possible and to destroy Hamas. Nothing is off the table. The best laid plans of mice, men, soldiers, and political leaders have gone awry.

This is a new beginning, and there is no assurance that it will have a happy ending.

In this short book, I analyze the current situation and its implications for the future of Israel and the world. It is necessarily a work in progress since events are moving so quickly and so unpredictably. I have been writing about this issue for nearly half a century. Much of what I have argued is still relevant, but new thinking is required. I hope to help stimulate such thinking.

CHAPTER 1

The Current War

A. The Attack

Israel is fighting a war not only for its own survival, but for the victory of humanity over barbarity. The Jewish people have long been the victims of barbarity, and the nation state of the Jewish people—now seventy-five years old—has been on the forefront of fighting for humanity.

The recent lynching, raping, beheading, and kidnapping of more than fourteen hundred Israelis—including American Jews—is only the most recent pogrom in a history that goes back millennia. The crusades, the inquisition, the Cossack massacres, the religiously inspired pogroms, and the Holocaust were all manifestations of the oldest continuing human prejudice—Jew hatred. Sometimes it has been religiously inspired. Other times it has been ethnically inspired; now under the pretext of anti-Zionism, it is ideologically inspired. The end result has always been the same: the massacres of Jewish babies, women, the elderly, and everyone else who fits within the ever-changing definition of "Jew."

Throughout history, the Jews have been the canary in the mineshaft, signaling the approach of more generalized hatreds against others, such as the Romanis, gays, and the handicapped during World War II.

Jew hatred rarely distinguishes on the basis of individual characteristics, such as religious observance, economic condition, ethnicity, or political perspective. During the Holocaust, Catholic priests were murdered if they had at least one Jewish grandparent. Stalin's campaign against Jewish intellectuals targeted Communists as well as anti-communist. The recent barbarity in Israel resulted in the murder of many pro-Palestinian, pro-peace, and pro-two-state solution left-wing opponents of the current Israeli government. To the Jew haters who engage in violence, the only thing that matters is whether you fit their criteria for being a Jew. That alone makes you a target.

The Hamas massacres were not designed to bring about a two-state solution, to end the occupation of the West Bank, or to achieve peace. Indeed, part of the motivation was to prevent any resolution of the conflict that left Israel standing. The goal was similar to the Nazi goal in the late 1930s and early 1940—judenrein—free of Jews. According to Hamas, the ancient land of Israel has to be ethnically cleansed of all Jews, either by murdering them or chasing them out. Now, American anti-Semites on university campuses are echoing the Nazi mantra of "cleansing" the world of Jews. They are holding up signs demanding "Keep the World Clean," illustrated by a Star of David being placed in a garbage pail.

Nor was the recent barbarity about making life better for Palestinians. Indeed, nothing could be worse for most Palestinians, than to be living under a Hamas or Hezbollah califate. Prior to the recent war in Gaza, Hamas controlled the 140-square mile area and made life miserable for its two million residents. When Israel ended its occupation in 2005—with the withdrawal of every single Israeli soldier and civilian—the Gaza Strip could have become the Singapore on the Mediterranean. The Israelis left behind farming equipment, hot houses, and gardens. Several European countries pledged fortunes of money to build up the strip. But shortly thereafter, Hamas engaged in a bloody coup against the Palestinian Authority and murdered and exiled their remaining leaders. It murdered gays, religious dissenters, and political opponents. It took complete control over every aspect of life in the cities and the countryside, causing poverty, unemployment, health issues, illiteracy, and other problems for the residents. Many Gazans nonetheless support Hamas, while others do not, but are fearful to expose their opposition.

During the course of the recent attacks, many university students, faculty, administrator and alumni sought to justify the lynching, raping, torturing, and kidnapping of Jewish Israeli civilians on the ground that "settlers are not civilians." They also argue that all means are justified when the end is to recover territory occupied by colonialists. It is important to understand what these arguments mean in the context of the recent events.

First, the victims of these massacres were living in Israel proper, not in areas captured in the 1948 or 1967 defensive wars. So they cannot be regarded as "settlers," except by those who believe that every inch of Israel is occupied by "settlers." In other words, every Jewish Israeli—even those descendants from Sephardic families that have lived in Eretz Yisrael (the ancient land of Israel) since before the birth of Muhammad—are settlers, and the areas in which their families lived since biblical times (such as Safad, Bnei Brak, and Jerusalem) are illegally occupied, simply because Jews live there.

They even claim that land on which no Jewish settler lives, such as the Gaza Strip, is "occupied," because following the illegal and bloody coup by Hamas against the Palestinian Authority in 2007, Israel has taken military steps necessary to prevent the firing of rockets and the deployment of terror tunnels against its civilians who Hamas have been targeting for more than fifteen years. The recent rocket attacks, incursions, and massacres prove the need for even greater protective measures and self-defense. Yet, within Gaza itself there are no Israeli soldiers or "settlers." When Israelis left Gaza, they even unburied their dead and took the bodies with them. By what rational definition is that an occupation?

To be sure, there is a continuing military occupation of some areas of the West Bank. And there are civilian settlements. The latter is controversial—both inside and outside of Israel—and justifies debate and even protest, but certainly not the massacre of civilians.

But one point is crystal clear: these massacres have little to do with the occupation of areas of the West Bank, or the failure to achieve a two-state solution. Hamas radicals would not be satisfied by the total end of the occupation of the West Bank and the withdrawal of all Jews from the areas subject to dispute—any more than they were satisfied with the withdrawal of all Jews, civilians, and soldiers from Gaza. To the contrary they doubled down on their terrorist attacks against civilians following the withdrawal.

The last thing Hamas wants is a two-state solution—or any solution that leaves Israel as the nation state of the Jewish people, regardless of how small it might be. They want a "final solution" akin to the deadly one sought by the Nazis.

But assume for a moment that Hamas were justified in all of its demands. Assume that Israel were a European colonialist bastion of white supremacy (despite Israel's heterogeneous population, multiracial population consisting mostly of people with Middle Eastern rather than European heritage). Assume even that Gaza is an open-air prison, despite the absence of any Israeli "prison guards" within its borders. Assume the worst that Hamas falsely alleges. Would any or even all of that justify what occurred in October of 2023?

Ben Shapiro addressed the question, after he was criticized for showing graphic pictures of the atrocities on his show:

> Here's the point. *Nothing anyone has ever done to you or could do to you would cause you to do these things.*
>
> No territorial dispute would cause you to butcher babies. No squabble over territory would cause you to rape and abduct women. No so-called "occupation" would cause you to kidnap entire families or burn them alive in their homes.
>
> The only type of person who would do something like this is a person who *isn't like you.* A person who *does not value life or children or decency* the same way that you do. A person who might proclaim they *love death like you love life.*
>
> Hamas is not like you.
>
> Those people who celebrate Hamas are not like you.
>
> And—Hamas *exploits the fact* that you are not like them. They murder your children, and they hide behind their own.
>
> They expect you to care *more about their kids than they do themselves.*
>
> But what's more important, they expect you to believe that they

care about their own children when they manifestly care more about other things. About destroying the state of Israel. About murdering every Jew in their bed.[1]

In this book I ask why so much of the world has been so morally bankrupt—so "eyeless in Gaza"—when it comes to the massacre of Israelis by Hamas, and Israeli efforts to prevent any recurrence. Why has there been so little moral clarity over this conflict between good and evil? Why does the media not do a better job of explaining that the dead Palestinian children it shows the world were killed because they were deliberately placed in harm's way by Hamas precisely in order to create these horrible images? Why is a double standard applied to Israeli self-defense actions? Why are the usual standards of criticism not applied to Hamas's double war crimes? Why are there so many more protests and so much more rage when the Israeli Army accidentally kills human shields in defense of its own children than when Muslims murder Jews and even other Muslims in cold blood and in much larger numbers throughout the world? Why is terrorism justified by so many only when it is directed at Israeli civilians? Why is so much of the world so wrong when it comes to Israel?

B. Israel Is Not a Colonial, Imperialist State

Among the most absurd but prevalent canards currently being promulgated against Israel—and used to justify Hamas barbarism—is that it is a colonial, imperialist, settler state, comparable to apartheid South Africa.

The reality is that Israel is a democracy comprising primarily of refugees and their descendants exercising their right to self-determination.

Beginning in the 1880s, the Jews who moved to what is now Israel were refugees escaping the oppressive anti-Semitism of colonial Europe and the Muslim states of the Middle East and North Africa.

---

1   Ben Shapiro, "Why I'm Showing You Hamas' Atrocities," *The Ben Shapiro Show*, October 11, 2023, YouTube, https://www.youtube.com/watch?v=SE5QG_BDUks&list=PLX_rhFRRlAG58_4z9KWPUYrnTM6QZDJrT&index=7

Unlike the colonial settlers serving the expansionist commercial and military goals of imperial nations such as Great Britain, France, the Netherlands, and Spain, the Jewish refugees were escaping from the countries that had oppressed them for centuries. These Jewish refugees were far more comparable to the American colonists who had left England because of religious oppression (or the Europeans who later immigrated to America) than they were to eighteenth- and nineteenth-century English imperialists who colonized India, the French settlers who colonized North Africa, and the Dutch expansionists who colonized Indonesia.

Those who absurdly claim that the Jewish refugees who immigrated to Palestine in the last decades of the nineteenth century were the "tools" of European imperialism must answer the following question: For whom were these socialists and idealists working? Were they planting the flag of the hated czar of Russia or the anti-Semitic regimes of Poland or Lithuania? These refugees wanted nothing to do with the countries from which they fled to avoid pogroms and religious discrimination. They came to what the Romans had named Palestine without any of the weapons of imperialism. They brought with them few guns or other means of conquest. Their tools were rakes and hoes. The land they cultivated was not taken away from its rightful owners by force or confiscation by colonial law. It was purchased, primarily from absentee landlords and real estate speculators, at fair or often exorbitant prices.

As Martin Buber, a strong supporter of Palestinian rights, observed in 1939: "Our settlers do not come here as do the colonists from the Occident, to have natives do their work for them; they themselves set their shoulders to the plow and they spend their strength and their blood to make the land fruitful."[2] Nor was the land they sought to cultivate rich in natural resources such as oil or gold, or strategically positioned as a trade route. It was a materially worthless piece of real estate in a backwater of the world whose significance to Jews was religious, historical, and familial.

---

2 "Martin Buber's Open Letter to Gandhi Regarding Palestine," https://www .jewishvirtuallibrary.org/martin-buber-s-open-letter-to-gandhi-regarding-palestine.

Clearly, these Jewish workers were not your typical imperialists. They were refugees from oppressive regimes who were seeking to begin new lives in a place their ancestors had long ago settled and from which most but not all of them had eventually been driven. Moreover, as the British historian Paul Johnson has documented, the colonial powers did everything possible to thwart the establishment of a Jewish homeland: "Everywhere in the West, the foreign offices, defense ministries, and big business were against the Zionists."[3] The Jewish refugees who came to live in Palestine had to overcome Turkish, British, and Pan-Arab imperialism and colonialism in order to achieve self-determination.

To prove beyond any reasonable doubt that Israel is not and has never been an imperialist or colonialist state, it is necessary to briefly recount the early history of the Jewish refugees from Europe who joined the mostly Sephardic Jews who had lived in Palestine for generations The first wave of immigration (or Aliyah as it was called), beginning in 1882 and ending in 1903, was not very different in many respects from the first large-scale immigration of Eastern European Jews to America at about the same time. This was an era of massive emigration and immigration throughout the world, especially from the crowded cities and towns of Europe. Enormous population shifts took place, with people settling in places far away from their birthplaces. Irish, Italian, Greek, German, Polish, and Jewish families as well as Chinese, Japanese, and Caribbean families, sought better lives in the United States, Canada, South America, Australia, and other places where they could work with their hands and develop their minds.

Approximately ten thousand Eastern European Jews immigrated to Palestine during that period as compared to nearly a million Jews who immigrated to the United States. The Jews of the First Aliyah produced a manifesto in 1882, in which they explicitly referred to the recent wave of pogroms as well as the more distant *auto-de-fé* that had threatened to destroy European Jewry. Like the Jews who

---

3   Paul Johnson, *Modern Times: The World from the Twenties to the Nineties* (New York: Harper & Row, 1983), 485.

sought refuge in America, most of the Jews who first returned to Zion were simply looking for a place to live in peace, without discrimination and without physical threats to their survival. They certainly had that right.

Palestine, the land of their forebears, seemed to be an appropriate place for several important reasons, including that there has always been a significant Jewish presence in Palestine.

The Crusaders massacred thousands of Jews along with Muslims in the eleventh century, but soon thereafter Jews from France, England, and later Spain, Lithuania, Portugal, Sicily, Sardinia, Rhodes, and Naples established centers of Jewish learning and commerce. From this time on, Palestine was never without a significant and well-documented Jewish presence. By the time the Ottoman Turks occupied Palestine in 1516, approximately ten thousand Jews lived in the Safad region alone. In the sixteenth century according to British reports, "as many as 15,000 Jews" lived in Safad which was "a center of rabbinical learning." Many more Jews lived in Jerusalem, Hebron, Acre, and other locations. Jerusalem, in fact, has had a Jewish majority since the first population figures were gathered in the early nineteenth century, and, according to the British consul in Jerusalem, the Muslims of Jerusalem "scarcely exceed[ed] one quarter of the whole population." Jerusalem was a predominantly Jewish city well before the First Aliyah by European Jews. By the middle of the nineteenth century—thirty years before the Firsts Aliyah—Jews also constituted a significant presence, often a plurality or majority, in Safad, Tiberias, and several other cities and towns. Tel Aviv has been a predominantly Jewish city since European Jews founded it on sand dunes in 1909.

Although most of the Jews of the First Aliyah were secular to the core, their longing for Zion transcended theology and was an important aspect of Jewish history. Jews who lived outside of Palestine were referred to as the diaspora or the exiles. The Jewish people never abandoned their claim to return to the land from which so many of their ancestors had been forcibly driven.

At about the time the first wave of European Jewish refugees were immigrating to Palestine, other waves of Jewish refugees from

Muslim countries such as Yemen, Iraq, Turkey, and North Africa were also beginning to arrive in Palestine. These Arab Jews had little knowledge of political Zionism. They were simply returning home to escape persecution, having learned that the Ottoman Empire was permitting (or closing its eyes to) some Jewish immigration into Palestine. At the same time, many Arabs from what is now Syria, Lebanon, Jordan, and Egypt moved to Palestine—some to work in Jewish wineries and other businesses.

Based on the actual history of the Jewish refugees who immigrated to Palestine, the claim that Israel is a colonial or imperialist state is so farfetched that it simply serves to illustrate how language is willfully distorted in the service of a partisan agenda.

Contrast the Jewish presence in Palestine—or as the Jews called it "Eretz Yisrael," the land of Israel—to the lack of presence or history of English settlers sent to New Zealand by Great Britain as part of its colonial enterprise. New Zealand is a perfect example of a colonialist-settler state. Israel is not.

C. A Brief History of the Gaza Conflict

Let me begin to answer questions raised by recent events with a brief chronology that places the Gaza conflict in context.

On October 2, 2001, only three weeks after the terror attacks of September 11th, President George W. Bush announced that the United States supported the creation of a Palestinian state. It was a major milestone for the Palestinian cause, since no previous American administration had officially acknowledged a Palestinian state as an explicit goal of US foreign policy. The announcement was all the more remarkable, given that the US was still reeling in the wake of 9/11, and that Palestinian extremists were still using terror against Israelis to achieve their goals. Bush's announcement offered a unique opportunity to Palestinians to end the violence and begin building a new future. Hamas's response came a few weeks later, when it fired the first Qassam rocket at the Israeli town of Sderot. The Hamas website proudly proclaimed: "The Zionist army is afraid that the Palestinians will increase the range of the new rockets, placing the towns and villages in the [Zionist] entity in danger."[4] It was only the first of thousands of rockets that Hamas and other Palestinian terror organizations would fire in their relentless effort to kill Jews and destroy the peace process.

Rocket and mortar fire from the Gaza Strip increased in late 2004 and early 2005. There was a brief halt in March 2005, in the aftermath of Mahmoud Abbas's victory in the Palestinian presidential elections, and an agreement signed by the various Palestinian factions in Cairo to halt violence. Hamas and other organizations merely used the lull to rearm, however. In August of that year, Israel carried out its "disengagement" from Gaza, voluntarily withdrawing thousands of settlers and soldiers and completely ending the Israeli presence there. The hope was that Palestinians would use the end of Israeli occupation to build Gaza's economy and prepare it for political independence, along with the West Bank, as part of a Palestinian state. Private donors stepped in to buy the Israeli greenhouses that had been left behind, and hand them over to the Palestinian Authority. James Wolfenson, the former head of the World Bank, contributed $500,000 of his own money to the purchase.[5] But almost immediately after the disengagement, Hamas and other terror organizations renewed their rocket fire, launching a barrage of rockets at the Israeli towns of Sderot and Ashqelon. The immediate trigger was an accident during a Hamas "victory rally," in which a truck filled with weapons exploded in a Gaza refugee camp, killing nineteen Palestinians.[6] There was little media focus on, and no demonstrations against, these largely civilian deaths.

Rocket fire continued throughout the months that followed, though Israel was no longer occupying Gaza. In November 2005, Israel signed an agreement with the Palestinian Authority to open the Rafah crossing on the Egypt-Gaza border. The agreement was part of an effort to encourage trade and economic development in

4   Hamas website, quoted in "Rocket threat from the Gaza Strip, 2000–2007," Intelligence and Terrorism Information Center at the Israel Intelligence Heritage and Commemoration Center (IICC), December 2007, 33–34.

5   CNN.com, "Gaza Settlers' Greenhouses to be Handed to Palestinians," August 12, 2005, http://www.cnn.com/2005/WORLD/meast/08/12/gaza/index.html.

6   IICC, 40.

Gaza, and to increase the responsibilities of the Palestinian government for the welfare of the Palestinian people. And, indeed, the Rafah crossing remained open throughout the first half of 2006.[7] The border remained open despite Hamas's victory in the Palestinian legislative elections in January 2006 that caused deep worry in Israel and throughout the international community. The Middle East Quartet—comprised of the European Union, United Nations, United States, and Russia—warned the new Palestinian government that further aid would be conditional on its "commitment to the principles of non-violence, recognition of Israel, and acceptance of previous agreements and obligations."[8] With several weeks to go before the new Palestinian government would be sworn in, Hamas had time to consider those reasonable conditions. And it rejected every one of them. That decision, in turn, prompted the Quartet, and Israel, to cut off financial assistance to the Palestinian Authority, though Israel continued to supply electricity and water to Gaza.

Hamas had a chance to reconsider. Instead, it resumed its attacks. Only one rocket was launched against Israel in January 2006, while Palestinian elections were under way. But in February alone, forty-seven rockets were fired. By June, Hamas and other groups had launched hundreds of Quassams, as well as an Iranian-made Grad rocket. On June 25, Hamas launched an attack inside Israel, having tunneled under the border near the Kerem Shalom ("Vineyard of Peace") border crossing. In the ensuing battle, Hamas kidnapped an Israeli soldier named Gilad Shalit, whom it held incommunicado for several years in violation of the principles of the Third Geneva Convention. Following the kidnapping, Israel attacked terrorist targets in Gaza and closed the Rafah crossing. The closure was not an attempt to punish Palestinians for the election results five months before but was the direct consequence

---

7   B'Tselem, "The Gaza Strip after Disengagement," accessed February 15, 2009, http://btselem.org/English/Gaza_Strip/.

8   Statement by Middle East Quartet, January 30, 2006, <http://www.un.org/News/Press/docs/2006/sg2104.doc.htm>.

of Hamas's attack on Israel and was deemed necessary to protect Israel's security.

Even after Hamas abducted Shalit, the Gaza borders were not completely closed. The Rafah crossing was open for twenty-four days over the next six months, and some movement of people and goods—albeit restricted—was allowed. Throughout this time, rocket fire from the Gaza Strip continued to terrorize Israeli civilians. Still, the international community gave the Palestinian leaders another chance to meet the basic demands it had issued in January 2006. But the two main Palestinian factions—Fatah, which controlled the executive, and Hamas, which controlled the legislature—began fighting openly with each other. After extensive negotiations, the two parties agreed to a unity government, which was formed in March 2007. But the rockets continued to rain down—reaching a record high of 257 in May 2007—and in June 2007, Hamas launched a military coup against the Fatah executive, driving its leaders out of Gaza and killing more than one hundred of their fellow Palestinians, including many civilians. Again, little media focus and no protest marches. With the entire territory under its iron-fisted control, Hamas increased rocket attacks against Israel, with other Palestinian terror organizations joining in. These attacks accelerated dramatically after Israel and the exiled leaders of the Palestinian Authority—still legally governed by Fatah, in the eyes of the international community—signed an agreement in Annapolis, Maryland, in November 2007, pledging to work towards a two-state solution.

It was only after Hamas's illegal and illegitimate coup, and the heavy rocket attacks that followed, that Israel imposed more extensive restrictions on Gaza designed to prevent and deter rocket and other attacks. In January 2008—nearly two years after Hamas took power, and after thousands of rockets and mortars had fallen on Israel's southern towns—Israel began restricting fuel and electricity to Gaza, in accordance with a nuanced ruling by Israel's High Court of Justice. Still, it continued to allow fuel and humanitarian aid to enter and allowed Palestinians to enter Israel to receive medical treatment in Israeli hospitals. Israel did not want ordinary Palestinians to suffer and did all that it could to alleviate their living conditions while reducing Hamas's ability to function as a terrorist regime. And yet Hamas continued to smuggle weapons into Gaza via underground tunnels on the Egyptian border. More than two thousand rockets and mortars were launched from Gaza into Israel in the first six months of 2008. Finally, in June, Israel and Hamas began an Egyptian-brokered "period of calm," during which rocket fire, though greatly reduced, continued to strike Israeli towns. In December 2008, Hamas unilaterally declared that it would resume its attacks with full force—and it promptly did so when the period of calm expired, forcing Israel to respond with Operation Cast Lead.

Between 2009 and the October 7, 2023 attack, Hamas continued to send rockets and terrorists into Israel. The year 2014 saw some of the worst fighting, starting with rocket attacks at cities in the heartland in Israel and culminating in operation Protective Edge, in which more than two thousand Palestinians, many of them combatants, and sixty-seven Israeli soldiers and six civilians were killed.

In the runup to the 2023 massacre, things were relatively quiet, as they have been before previous Hamas attacks. Thousands of Gazans were permitted to enter Israel to work and bring back their salaries. It now turns out that some of these "workers" were actually Hamas spies who provided the terrorists information about the location of civilian targets and military facilities. Hamas always seeks to justify their aggression by pointing to some alleged provocation, most recently some tensions on the Temple Mount in Jerusalem, by a small number of religious extremists. But the October 7 invasion was planned well before any alleged provocation. The attack was obviously designed to thwart the peace process with Saudi Arabia and other states in the region.

D. The Hamas Playbook

The Hamas playbook in Gaza is clear to anyone who is not eyeless or morally oblivious: attack Israeli civilians; anticipate Israel's response by using human shields that assure that in its effort to target Hamas terrorist, Israel will cause collateral damage to Palestinian civilians;

seek condemnation by the international community and the media; demand a cease fire; use the cease fire to rearm and get ready for the next cycle.

Hamas itself has a name for this. They call it "the CNN strategy." (This is not to criticize CNN or any objective news source for doing its job; it is to criticize Hamas for exploiting the freedom of press that it forbids in Gaza). The CNN strategy works because decent people all over the world are naturally sickened by images of dead and injured children. When they see such images repeatedly flashed across TV screens, they tend to react emotionally, rather than asking why these children are dying and who is to blame for putting them in harm's way. Average viewers, regardless of their political or ideological perspective, want to see the killing stopped. They blame those whose weapons directly caused the deaths, rather than those who provoked the violence by deliberately targeting civilians and hiding behind human shields.

They forget the usual rules of morality and law. The use of human shields, in the way Hamas uses the civilian population of Gaza, is a war crime—as is its firing of rockets at Israeli civilians. Every human shield that is killed by Israeli self-defense measures is the responsibility of Hamas, but you wouldn't know that from watching the media coverage.

The CNN strategy also works because people have short memories. They don't see current events in the context of similar past events, so they fail to understand that what they are now seeing is a rerun of a tactic designed by Hamas to be repeated endlessly.

The CNN strategy seems to work better, at least in some parts of the world, against Israel that it would against other nations. There is much more protest—and fury—directed against Israel when it inadvertently kills civilians in a just war of self-defense, than against Arab and Muslim nations and groups that deliberately kill far more civilians for no legitimate reason.

It isn't the nature of the victims, since many more Arabs and Muslim civilians are killed in Africa and the Middle East by Arab and Muslim governments and groups with little or no protests.

It isn't the nature of the killings, since Israel goes to extraordinary lengths to avoid killing civilians—if for no other reason than that it hurts its cause—while Hamas does everything in its power to force Israel to kill Palestinian civilians by firing its missiles from densely populated civilian areas and refusing to build shelters for its civilians while building massive underground shelters for its leaders.

It isn't the nature of the conflict, either, because Israel is fighting a war of self-defense designed to protect its own civilians from rocket attacks and incursions, while most of those killed by Arabs and Muslims are killed in tribal warfare with no legitimate aim.

The world simply doesn't seem to care when Arabs and Muslims kill large numbers of other Arabs and Muslims, as occurred during the Black September Massacres conducted by Jordanians against Palestinians, but a qualitatively different standard applies when the Jewish state kills even a relatively small number of Muslims and Arabs in a war of self-defense.

The international community doesn't even seem to care when Palestinian children are killed by rocket fire—unless it is from Israeli rockets. In several instances, Hamas has fired anti-personnel rockets at Israeli civilians, but the rockets fell short of their target and killed Palestinian civilians. Yet there is virtually no coverage and absolutely no protests against these "collateral" civilian deaths, because Hamas refuses to allow TV cameras to show these dead Palestinian children. There was coverage of the recent explosion in a hospital parking lot only because it was falsely blamed on Israel.

Nor have there been protests against the cold-blooded murders by Hamas and its supporters of dozens of Palestinian civilians who allegedly "collaborated" with Israel. Indeed, Hamas and other terrorist groups, along with Arab countries, have killed far more Palestinian civilians than have the Israelis, but you wouldn't know that from the media, the United Nations, or protesters who focus selectively on only those deaths caused by Israeli military actions.

The protesters who fill the streets of New York, London, Paris, and San Francisco are nowhere to be seen when Jewish children are murdered by Palestinian terrorists.

Moreover, the number of civilians killed by Israel is almost always exaggerated, as President Biden has asserted. First, it is widely

assumed that if a victim is a "child" or a "woman," he or she is necessarily a civilian.

But Hamas often uses fourteen-, fifteen-, sixteen-, and seventeen-
year-olds, as well as women, as terrorists. Israel is entitled under international law to treat these "children" and women as the combatants
they have become. Hamas cannot, out of one side of its mouth, boast
that it recruits children and women to become terrorists, and then,
out of the other side of its mouth, complain when Israel takes it at its
word. The media should look closely and critically at the number of
claimed civilian victims before accepting self-serving and self-con-
tradictory exaggerations. Instead, it repeats the misleading "statistic"
that half of Gaza's population is comprised of "children," without
informing the public that many of these "children" shoot guns, build
terror tunnels, fire missiles, and kidnap Israeli children and babies.

By any objective count, the number of genuinely innocent
civilians killed by the Israeli Air Force in Gaza is lower than the
collateral deaths caused by other nations in comparable situations.
Hamas does everything in its power to provoke Israel into killing as
many Palestinian civilians as possible, in order to generate condemnation against the Jewish state. It has gone so far as firing rockets
from Palestinian schoolyards and hiding its terrorists in Palestinian
maternity wards. Immediately following the barbarism of October
7, many of the barbarians sought shelter in hospitals, schools, and
mosques.

The reality is that the elected and de facto government of Gaza
has declared war against Israel. Under Article 51 of the United
Nations Charter, it has committed an "armed attack" against Israel.
The Hamas charter calls for Israel's total destruction. Under international law, Israel is entitled to take whatever military action is
necessary to repel that attack and stop the rockets.

It must seek to minimize civilian deaths consistent with the
legitimate military goal, and it is doing precisely that, despite
Hamas's efforts to maximize civilian deaths on both sides. As
Golda Meir long ago put it: "We can forgive the Arabs for killing
our children, but we can never forgive them for forcing us to kill
their children."

E. University Responses

Even before Israel responded militarily to the massacre of October 7, 2023, American supporters of Hamas in the United States and around the world were blaming Israel for the mass murder of its own civilians and children.

Student groups at Harvard, Yale, City University of New York, Columbia, and other major institutions of learning issued statements in support of the Hamas murderers and rapists. Hundreds of students at Harvard issued the following blood libel on behalf of more than thirty organizations including Amnesty International at Harvard:

"We the undersigned student organizations hold the Israeli regime entirely responsible for all unfolding violence . . . the apartheid regime is the only one to blame."

Similar statements were issued by student groups around the country. Many faculty members and administrators support—indeed encourage—such bigotry. This was even before Israel even responded to the mass murder of its civilians.

This should not be surprising in light of the propaganda demonizing Israel that has flooded university campuses for decades. Speakers such as Norman Finkelstein have become among the most popular supporters of Hamas's genocidal goals.

While Israeli babies, women, and elderly civilians were being butchered, this despicable bigot and Holocaust minimizer published the following:

> If we honor the Jews who revolted in the Warsaw Ghetto—then moral consistency commands that we honor the heroic resistance in Gaza. I, for one, will never begrudge—on the contrary, it warms every fiber of my soul—the scenes of Gaza's smiling children as their arrogant Jewish supremacist oppressors have finally been humbled.[9]

---

9   Norman Finkelstein, "John Brown's Body—in Gaza," Norman Finkelstein's official Substack, October 7, 2023, https://normanfinkelstein.substack.com/p /john-browns-body-in-gaza.

The comparison is obscene. In the Warsaw uprising, brave civilians arose against well-armed Nazi soldiers who were trying to kill them. The only murders and rapes were by the Stormtroopers. In Israel, the murderers and rapists were the Hamas butchers who warm Mr. Finkelstein's soul.

Despite, perhaps because of, these outrageous, immoral, and historically inaccurate defamations, Mr. Finkelstein will continue to be invited to speak to large audiences at our major universities, while pro-Israel speakers—even those like me who support a two-state peaceful solution—will continue to be banned.

It is outrageous that hard-left woke progressives who claim to support women's rights are in the forefront of defending rapists who parade their bleeding victims. Many of the Israelis who were murdered at the peace concert and at nearby kibbutzim supported a two-state solution and the rights of innocent Palestinians.

This doesn't matter to the genocidal Hamas murderers and their supporters. All that matters is that the victims were Jews—Israeli Jews, American Jews, British Jews. The goal of these murderers is not a two-state solution or a peaceful resolution of the Middle East conflict.

No, it is the murder of Israel's population and of Jews around the world who support the only nation-state of the Jewish people. It is bigotry pure and simple, and according to these bigots, anyone who supports the Jewish state deserves the most extreme condemnation in the court of public opinion.

The most troubling aspect of these university statements in support of rapists and murderers is that many who signed them will be our future leaders. The universities that admitted and teach them have historically turned-out future members of Congress, presidents, economic leaders, journalists, and others who will determine the fate of our children and grandchildren. These universities have failed our future.

The disgusting, but predictable public defense of Hamas by so many students has generated a debate in universities about whether and how to respond to students who support, defend, or even praise what Hamas terrorists deliberately did to innocent Israeli children, the elderly and other civilians.

On the one hand there are considerations of free speech and academic freedom. As the president of Harvard, Claudine Gay, put it in refusing to condemn the more than thirty student groups who blamed Israel alone for the Hamas horrors: "Harvard embraces a commitment to free expression."

That would be acceptable if the university had a strict and consistent policy of never taking positions on issues that do not directly involve the university. The University of Chicago takes that position. Harvard does not. Former Harvard president Lawrence Summers reminded the current Harvard administration that Harvard has forfeited that prerogative—to "pursue a policy of neutrality"—by speaking out on other issues such as the killing of George Floyd.

The testing question would be: What if anything would Harvard's current president have said if a group of Harvard clubs had blamed the lethal firebombing of a Black church on the burned Black children or on the NAACP? What if they blamed the shooting up of a gay bar on the lifestyles of the murdered gays? Or the lynching of Blacks on their "uppity" attitudes?

We know what the reaction of university administrators would have been. At the very least, they would have exercised their own freedom of expression to condemn these groups in the strongest terms.

So, I have two direct questions to President Gay (who I like personally): 1) Would you have refused to condemn student groups that took these despicable positions, citing their freedom of expression? 2) If you would have condemned such groups (as I am confident you would have) how do you distinguish these groups from those you have refused to condemn? Is supporting the mass murder of Jews any less deserving of condemnation than the supporting of those who burn churches, shoot gays, or lynch Blacks? How then can you justify not condemning the Harvard groups?

Is it because you would be criticized for condemning pro-Hamas students but praised for condemning anti-Black and anti-gay bigots? That is not a principled basis for making a distinction. What then is the basis?

Certainly not Harvard's sordid history which is rife with both racism and anti-Semitism.

For generations Harvard excluded or limited the number of Jewish students. In the 1930s it honored German Nazis. As recently as when I arrived there in 1964, it discriminated against Jews in the selection of presidents and deans. It welcomed recruitment on campus by corporations and law firms that openly discriminated against Jews.

To its credit, Harvard has tried to reckon with its history of anti-Black racism. It must now reckon with its history of anti-Semitism and its current application of double standards in tolerating Jew hatred among elements of its student body, faculty, and administrators.

It is no excuse to say that the current Jew hatred is directed at the nation state of the Jewish people rather than at Jews as a group. Hamas lynched, raped, beheaded, and kidnapped Jews who lived in Israel. They have murdered non-Israeli Jews in other parts of the world, and their charter is filled with anti-Jewish canards borrowed from the notorious anti-Semitic forgery, the *Protocols of the Elders of Zion*. Hamas is a Jew-hating, anti-Semitic terrorist group, and students who support it by shifting the blame from them to the Jews of Israel are complicit in Hamas's Jew hatred and must be held accountable.

Nor is it an excuse or justification that the offending groups are comprised of young students, some of whom claim they didn't realize what they are signing. They knew they were signing an anti-Israel petition at a time when Israeli Jews were being slaughtered. The fact that some may have signed it without reading it only goes to show the knee-jerk hatred of some students toward anything involving Israel or Jews. They would never have signed a petition critical of gays or Blacks without studying it carefully.

Harvard treats its students—both eighteen-year-old freshmen or twenty-five-year-old graduate students_as adults, holding them responsible for what they write or sign. They do not excuse plagiarism even if negligent. There is no basis for an exception here. Students who supported this and similar petitions should be called out and criticized. If they want to retract their signatures they should do so publicly and apologize. Silence is complicity. Freedom of expression precludes the power to punish immoral speech. But it includes the right to condemn such speech. President Gay must condemn these offending students in the strongest terms.

Much of the blame lies with the faculty and administration of elite universities, which have taken strong views against racism, sexism, homophobia, and other forms of bigotry, while remaining silent about the oldest prejudice, anti-Semitism, which today disguises itself as anti-Zionism. Jews and Zionists are not included among minorities who deserve protection.

Among the Harvard groups most prominently blaming Israel for these rapes and murders is Amnesty International at Harvard. That group is the Harvard affiliate of the Nobel Prize-winning international organization that claims to be in favor of peace and nonviolence. (After receiving protest, Amnesty removed its name.)

I don't know whether the Harvard affiliate represents the views of its parent organization, but Amnesty International has failed, at least so far, to disassociate itself from these abhorrent anti-peace and pro-violence views. Nor has Harvard University, with which these groups boast an association, condemned them.

None of these major universities would allow a Ku Klux Klan, white supremicist, or other anti-Black, anti-gay, anti-woman organization to be associated with the university. Whatever these universities would do with regard to such other bigoted groups, they must do with regard to these bigoted groups.

This is not about politics. This is about supporting murderers and rapists of Jews. These bigots must not be allowed to hide behind political claims. When a single African American named George Floyd was brutally and unjustifiably murdered by police, this caused a major "reckoning" at American universities and other institutions.

Billions of dollars and other resources were redirected at remedying anti-Black bigotry. The time has come for a new reckoning—a reckoning by American universities with their own tolerance and even encouragement of anti-Semitism and anti-Zionism.

The immoral groups that support Hamas atrocities are composed of students, faculty members, and administrators. Many of these individuals hide behind their organizations' names and refuse to identify themselves. They do not want to be held accountable in the court of public opinion for their own despicable views.

The open marketplace of ideas, which I support, allows students to hold and express these views, but it also requires transparency so that the rest of us can judge them, hold them accountable, and debate them.

There are, of course, rare occasions where anonymity is essential. For example, during the civil rights period of the 1960s, identifying members of civil rights groups endangered their lives. There is, however, no such fear here. Groups that oppose Hamas have not been known to advocate violence against those who support it. To the contrary, it is pro-Israel advocates who have been threatened with and suffered from violence.

The students who anonymously vote to support Hamas's recent attacks need not be fearful of anything but disdain and criticism. They should be willing to subject themselves to the marketplace of ideas. They should not resort to cowardly hiding behind the names of prominent organizations such as Amnesty International at Harvard. (As noted, after receiving protest, Amnesty removed its name.)

Some students who belong to these organizations argue that they do not personally support Hamas's recent barbarities. They are free to say so and to dissociate themselves from the groups they voluntarily joined. Silence in this context is acquiescence. So is hiding behind anonymity.to defend these immoral views.

Fellow students, future employers, and others should be able to judge their friends and potential employees by the views they have expressed. Teachers should not grade students based on their views. That is why anonymous grading is widely employed at universities.

As a university professor for fifty years, I would not grade down a student because she supported Hamas atrocities. Nor would I befriend or employ such a student. Freedom of speech is not freedom from being held accountable for one's speech. It is interesting that most of the counterpetitions protesting Hamas's activities contain the names of students and faculty, but that is far less true of petitions that support Hamas's atrocities. That is understandable because there is no reasonable defense for what Hamas has done. Those who support Hamas should be ashamed and shamed, and those who oppose Hamas should be praised. That, too, is part of the marketplace of ideas.

Today, too many students are judged by their "identity." Identity politics has replaced meritocracy. Being judged by one's support or opposition to Hamas barbarity is more justifiable.

Let the student newspapers, many of which are rabidly anti-Israel, publish the names of all students and faculty members who belong to groups that support and oppose Hamas. Hypothetically, if a club were formed at any of these universities that advocated rape or the lynching of African Americans, the newspapers would most assuredly publish the names of everyone associated with such a despicable group. Why is this different? Rape has become a weapon of war for Hamas, along with lynching, mutilation, mass murder, and kidnapping. Expressing support for these acts, while constitutionally protected, is wrong. The answer to wrong speech isn't censorship; it is right speech, and transparency.

So let the names be published. Let the despicable students and faculty members who support Hamas stand up and defend their indefensible views and let the marketplace of ideas decide who is right and who is wrong.

F. Lawyer Responses

Within a day of the brutal massacre of Israeli babies, women, the elderly and others, the National Lawyers Guild issued a statement in support of the mass murderers. The National Lawyers Guild is a group of hard-left lawyers, students, and legal workers. It has branches in law schools throughout the country and has many members, especially among law students.

It began as a liberal organization before World War II and included many legal luminaries, including Jews. But quickly it was taken over by the Communist Party, and it supported the Hitler-Stalin Pact of 1939. As a result of its support for Hitler, many liberal members quit. But committed communists who always follow the party line remained members. Following World War II, it again attracted some liberals who saw it as an alternative to the conservative American

Bar Association. But then in the 1970s, it was taken over by radical leftists, including some communists. It was no longer a home for liberals.

In 1948, the guild followed the lead of the Soviet Union in supporting the establishment of Israel. But when the Soviet Union and the Communist Party turned against Israel in the 1960s, the guild followed suit in opposing Israel and supporting Palestinian terrorists. Nonetheless, some liberals, including Jews, remained members. It remains to be seen whether it will lose the support of Jewish liberals, following the events of October 7, 2023.

It is important to note that the lengthy statement by the Lawyer's Guild in support of Hamas and in opposition to Israel was issued before Israel responded to the Hamas attack. It was posted on October 8, while bodies were still being recovered from the south of Israel.

The statement described the rapes, beheadings, murders, and kidnappings committed by Hamas as "the recent military actions carried out by Palestinian resistance . . ." It urged the public to support resistance to Israel's occupation "by all available means including armed struggle," by which they included rapes and beheadings. It criticized those who had condemned Hamas's barbarity. It accused Israel of genocide and demanded that Hamas be removed from the United States list of foreign terrorist organizations. It demanded that Israel be held legally accountable for the defense of its citizens. It mendaciously claimed that Israel's goal is to "annihilate" the Palestinians, and it demanded the release of every single Palestinian prisoner—including those convicted of mass murder. It did not call for the release of the hostages held by Hamas, and it opposed efforts of any country to "normalize relations with Israel." It said not a single word in condemnation of the rapes, beheadings, and kidnappings of Israeli babies, children, and women.

I am not aware of any law school in which the National Lawyers Guild has a chapter condemning or even criticizing this statement, which was not produced from thin air or by artificial intelligence; it was written and circulated by specific leaders of the National Lawyers Guild, including students at America's leading universities.

Students who support this outrageously anti-Semitic, anti-American, and anti-humanitarian statement are currently being given job offers by America's leading law firms, by government agencies, by hedge funds and by other potential employers. I am sure that many of these employers are unaware that they may be hiring lawyers who support the rapes and beheading of Jewish women and children. Full transparency, which lies at the core of the marketplace of ideas protected by the First Amendment, demands that the name of every member of the National Lawyers Guild who supports this statement be made public, so that potential employers know who they are hiring. Few clients would be willing to be represented by lawyers who have advocated the rape, beheading, murder, and kidnapping of Jewish civilians.

If there were groups of law students at any law school that advocated the lynching of African Americans, the raping of women or the killing of gay and transgender people, the National Lawyers Guild would be the first to demand that the names of the students supporting such atrocities be made public. Now the shoe is on the other foot, and it is the Guild that is supporting such barbarity.

Publicizing the names and law schools of students who support Hamas violence against civilians is not "doxxing." It does not disclose private information about their home addresses, their sexual preferences, or anything else other than their names. These students have identified themselves as members of the National Lawyers Guild. They are adults and are responsible for their actions and inactions.

Publishing their names serves the interest of truth and transparency. And so, I intend to publish—on my website, my podcast, and in my op-eds—the names of any student who signed or supported the bigoted statement of the National Lawyers Guild.

G. An Open Letter to Law Firms That Hire Hamas Supporters

Do your clients want to be represented by lawyers who support the designated terrorist organization Hamas? Do they want lawyers who approve of rapes, beheadings, and kidnappers of Israeli Jews? Do they want lawyers who have harassed and threatened Jews? Do your clients have a right to know whether such bigots work for your law firm so they can decide for themselves whether they want to be represented by them?

Some law firms have withdrawn offers from law students who blamed the Hamas mass murders on Israel alone. Indeed, a consortium of law firms has sent a letter to the deans of US law schools saying that "as employers who recruit from each of your law schools, we look to you to ensure your students [that our firms] have zero tolerance policies for any form of discrimination or harassment, much less the kind that has been taking place on some law school campuses." Others law firms have remained silent. As a teacher of legal ethics, I believe that law firms that hire such supporters of Hamas barbarism have an ethical obligation to disclose the decision they have made to their clients, and to not assign such lawyers to any client without getting their informed consent.

If the students or lawyers recant their earlier support, as some appear to have done, that fact, too, should be disclosed, but the clients should be informed that they originally supported the Hamas barbarities. It is up to the client, not the law firm, to decide what weight, if any, to give to any alleged recantation.

Consider the case of Ibrahim Bharmal, a law review student at Harvard Law School, where I taught students like him for fifty years. Numerous sources have identified him from a video as one of the students who harassed a Jewish student, surrounding him, shouting at him, and preventing him from leaving a situation that he believed was threatening to him physically. Some reports say the harassers were "grabbing and shoving him to the ground," and that Bharmal was among the leaders of the group.

Bharmal was also reportedly the co-president of the South Asian Law Student Association (SALSA), which joined a public statement released the day after the Hamas rapes, beheadings, and kidnapping, blaming all these atrocities entirely on Israel. This statement was issued before Israel counterattacked Hamas in Gaza. After receiving much criticism, SALSA issued another statement seeking to retract the first one.

In light of his status as a law review editor, it is highly likely that Bharmal has received numerous job offers, almost certainly from employers who were unaware of his actions. Now that they have been made public by his participation in the videotaped harassment and the published original petitions, as well as the public retraction, what should employers who made job offers do? They certainly should provide him with the opportunity to explain his specific roles in the harassment, original petition, and retraction. But whatever a given law firm decides, it would be ethically obliged to notify potential clients of all the facts regarding the Hamas supporting lawyer assigned to represent a client.

The same is true of any lawyer who is an active member of the National Lawyers Guild, a hard-left organization that supported the Hamas atrocities, declaring them to be appropriate "military "responses to Israel's occupation. So did the Bronx Defender union, which represents indigent clients.

If a lawyer belongs to the National Lawyers Guild, the Bronx Public Defenders, or other legal organizations that support Hamas, clients should be entitled to ask them whether they support the barbaric acts committed by that terror group on October 7. Some will probably say they were unaware that their organization supported the Hamas atrocities. Others may say they support Hamas—despite its designation as a terror group to whom it is criminal to provide material support—but not these specific acts. While still others will try to justify the atrocities as appropriate military responses to an occupation.

Clients have the right to know which of these (or other) positions a lawyer selected to represent them espouses. Many clients will not want to be represented by a lawyer who believes that the rapes and beheadings of civilians, including children, are appropriate military actions. Others may.

In any event, clients are entitled to have the information to help make the decision.

It is important to understand that holding individual lawyers accountable for public actions and petitions is not "doxxing," as some have claimed. The marketplace of ideas, protected by the First Amendment, requires transparency, which generally includes knowing the identity of those who participate in that marketplace. Doxxing involves disclosing information that was intended to remain private, such as sexual preferences, home addresses, and the identity and location of family members. It does not involve disclosing merely the names of individuals who participated in harassment or who supported publicly issued statements.

Students and lawyers have a First Amendment right to espouse outrageous and immoral views—just as the neo-Nazis did when they marched through Skokie—without fear of punishment by the government. But private clients also have a right to evaluate their potential lawyers on the basis of how they exercise that right.

H. Israel's Difficult Options

Israel has declared northern Gaza a war zone. They have given its civilians the opportunity to move several miles south in order to protect themselves from Israeli bombing of legitimate military targets, including Gaza City. Hamas has told the civilians to stay and serve as human shields. It is actually blocking the egress roads to safety so as to assure that civilians who want to leave cannot do so.

The feckless United Nations, instead of helping with evacuation, has told the civilians that evacuation is "impossible."

No, it isn't.

It may be logistically difficult and imperfect, but many civilian lives could be saved if the UN and other groups, such as the Red Cross and Red Crescent, were to try to help families to move out of harm's way. But Hamas wants these human shields—especially children, women, and the elderly—to remain in harm's way. It is not enough for them that the more than two hundred Israeli hostages already serve the same purpose. Moreover, it is firing rockets from the south in order to induce Israel to target those launching areas, so that civilians who have gone south will be killed.

Using the most vulnerable of civilians in this way is a Hamas tactic that goes back many years. As one of its leaders boasted in 2008: "For the Palestinian people, death has become an industry. . . . The elderly excel at this, and so do . . . the children. This is why they have formed human shields of the women and children."

This boast has been repeated over the years in the form of the Hamas slogan, "We love death as our enemy loves life," as has the use of children as human shields to protect legitimate military targets against lawful Israeli bombing. In giving civilians sufficient warning to leave, Israel has gone further than other Western nations at war. In World War II, the US did not give meaningful warnings to the civilians of Japanese cities (Hiroshima and Nagasaki) that were about to be the targets of nuclear or firebombing attacks (Tokyo). Great Britain did not give the civilians of Dresden the opportunity to leave. In more recent wars—such as Vietnam, Iraq, and Afghanistan—advance warnings were rarely provided before bombs were dropped.

Israel is generally held to a higher standard of morality by other governments, the media, and academia. Hamas knows this and exploits it as a weapon of war. Hamas understands that the killing of civilians—whether deliberate or collateral to legitimate military actions—is seen as wrong. But when dead children are shown on TV, many viewers fail to distinguish between deliberate targeting of civilians and unintentional collateral deaths. Hamas takes advantage of this psychological reality.

Israel must not permit itself to be limited in its preventive military actions by the double standard of morality imposed upon it by many and taken advantage of by Hamas. It is an all-out war against Hamas-controlled Gaza, and Israel is entitled, by any fair reading of international law, to do to Gaza City what the US did to Berlin and Tokyo in 1945. It has warned civilians to leave, and if they choose to remain, as many have, or if they are prevented from leaving by Hamas, this cannot be allowed to stop Israel from accomplishing its legitimate preventive goals. The collateral deaths of Palestinian civilians, caused directly by the Hamas decision to use them as human shields, is the moral, political, and legal responsibility of Hamas.

For far too long, Israel has been deterred from taking necessary military action by its concern about violating the double standards imposed on it by friends and foes alike. Indeed, Israeli reluctance to violate those standards allowed Hamas to re-arm and re-coordinate its military to facilitate the recent horrible massacres.

These brutal attacks against Israeli civilians must change all that. Israel should apply its own very high standards of morality in deciding how to balance the collateral deaths of Palestinian civilians against the need to prevent the intended deaths of its own civilians at the hands of Hamas. It should resolve doubts in favor of its civilians, as all nations throughout history have done.

I. Are Hamas Shields Civilians?

The news is filled with reports of civilian casualties, comparative civilian body counts, and criticism of Israel for causing the deaths, injuries and "collective punishment" of civilians. But just who is a "civilian" in the age of terrorism, when militants don't wear uniforms, don't belong to regular armies, and easily blend into civilian populations?

We need a new vocabulary to reflect the realities of modern warfare. A new phrase should be introduced into the reporting and analysis of current events in the Middle East: "the continuum of civilianality" (or the continuum of culpability). Though cumbersome, this concept aptly captures the reality and nuance of warfare today and provides a more fair way to describe those who are killed, wounded, and punished.

There is a vast difference—both moral and legal—between a two-year-old who is killed by an enemy rocket and a thirty-year-old civilian who has allowed his house to be used to store Katyusha rockets. Both are technically civilians, but the former is far more innocent than the latter. There is also a difference between a civilian who merely favors or even votes for a terrorist group and one who provides financial or other material support for terrorism.

Finally, there is a difference between civilians who are held hostage against their will by terrorists who use them as involuntary human shields, and civilians who voluntarily place themselves in harm's way in order to protect terrorists from enemy fire.

These differences and others are conflated within the increasingly meaningless word *civilian*—a word that carried great significance when uniformed armies fought other uniformed armies on battlefields far from civilian population centers. Today this same word equates the truly innocent with guilty accessories to terrorism.

The domestic law of crime, in virtually every nation, reflects this continuum of culpability. For example, in the infamous Fall River rape case (fictionalized in the film *The Accused*), there were several categories of morally and legally complicit individuals: those who actually raped the woman; those who held her down; those who blocked her escape route; those who cheered and encouraged the rapists; and those who could have called the police but did not.

No rational person would suggest that any of these people were entirely free of moral guilt, although reasonable people might disagree about the legal guilt of those in the last two categories. Their accountability for rape is surely a matter of degree, as is the accountability for terrorism of those who work with the terrorists.

It will, of course, be difficult for international law—and for the media—to draw the lines of subtle distinction routinely drawn by domestic criminal law. This is because domestic law operates on a retail basis—one person and one case at a time. International law and media reporting about terrorism tend to operate on more of a wholesale basis—with body counts, civilian neighborhoods, and claims of collective punishment.

But the recognition that "civilianality" is often a matter of degree, rather than a bright line, should still inform the assessment of casualty figures in wars involving terrorists, paramilitary groups, and others who fight without uniforms—or help those who fight without uniforms.

Turning specifically to the current fighting between Israel and Hamas, the line between Israeli soldiers and civilians is relatively clear. Hamas rockets target and hit Israeli restaurants, apartment buildings, and schools. They are loaded with anti-personnel ball bearings designed specifically to maximize civilian casualties. The massacres of October 7 clearly targeted civilians.

Hamas terrorists, on the other hand, are difficult to distinguish from those "civilians" who recruit, finance, harbor, and facilitate their terrorism. Nor can women and children always be counted as civilians, as some organizations do. Terrorists increasingly use women and teenagers to play important roles in their attacks.

The Israeli army has given well-publicized notice to civilians to leave those areas of southern Lebanon that have been turned into war zones. Those who voluntarily remain behind have become complicit. Some—those who cannot leave on their own—should be counted among the innocent victims.

If the media were to adopt this "continuum," it would be informative to learn how many of the "civilian casualties" fall closer to the line of complicity and how many fall closer to the line of innocence.

Every civilian death is a tragedy, but some are more tragic than others.

The long-practiced Hamas strategy of using Palestinian children and other civilians as human shields raises the important and old moral issue of weighing the lives of enemy civilians against the lives of one's own civilians and soldiers. Even if some of the Palestinian "civilians" are not entirely innocent, and even if their deaths were unintended and collateral to legitimate military objectives, they are tragic. As I have argued, Israel has a right under international law to prefer preventing the deaths of its own civilians over inadvertently causing the deaths of enemy civilians.

No such moral calculus is available to measure the cost to Israel of inadvertently causing the deaths of its own citizens who are illegally and immorally being held as hostages and used as human shields in their legitimate efforts to prevent future attacks to its civilians and current attacks on its soldiers. This is more a tactical than a moral issue, though it contains elements of both. But it involved complex decisions that Israel alone is entitled, indeed obligated to make. No international law or claims of universal morality have a say, because the balance here is between the lives of Israeli hostages and Israeli values.

How then should Israel weigh the lives of the hostages against those of its soldiers and its future civilian victims? There is no clear answer provided by history, morality, military tactics, or any other body of knowledge and experience. But a few generalizations may be relevant and instructive.

Civilian lives of one's citizens are valued more than military lives. This is because the role of the soldier includes risking his or her life in the interest of protecting its citizens. This may not be as obvious in a nation like Israel with near universal conscription. For example, is the life of a conscripted soldier less valuable than the life of a Yeshiva student who refused to be conscripted to help his country? These and other micro questions do not detract from the macro answer that when a tragic choice must be made between the life of a soldier and a civilian, all other things being equal, the civilian life should be preferred.

But all things are never equal, especially in the fog of war, or even in the planning of war from headquarters distant from the battlefield. Tactical and strategic considerations may require the sacrifice of civilian lives. The story of Churchill's decision regarding the German bombing of Coventry, whether completely true, partially true, or apocryphal illustrates the dilemma.

Historians have long debated whether Churchill was aware of but refused to warn the residents of Coventry to get out of the way of the Luftwaffe bombing that caused six hundred civilian deaths, because such a warning would have disclosed to the Germans that the British had cracked the German Enigma Code. This disclosure would have caused the deaths of many British soldiers who were relying on intelligence secured from Enigma, which would have dried up if the German's knew it was compromised.

Of course, every civilian death in Coventry was entirely the fault of the Nazis, legally, morally, and politically, just as every death to an Israeli hostage used as a human shield would be the fault of Hamas, regardless of who actually fired the fatal shot. But this doesn't solve the problem for Israeli policymakers, generals, or soldiers of how much risk to their own civilian hostages should they be willing to take to achieve their legitimate military goals.

To paraphrase Yitzhak Rabin: Israel should try to negotiate the freedom of hostages as if there were no ground war and should pursue the ground war as if there were no hostages. The latter is a lot more difficult to accomplish than the former because Hamas's unlawful use of Israeli civilian hostages imposes logistical restrictions on the military options available on the ground.

The bottom line is that Israel should be free to strike whatever balance it seems appropriate. It will, of course, do everything it can to preserve the lives of the hostages, while Hamas will do everything it can to use the hostages as weapons against the Israeli military. It will not be easy, but it must be done.

J. The Phony War Crimes Accusation against Israel

Every time Israel seeks to defend its civilians against terrorist attacks, it is accused of war crimes by various United Nations agencies, hard-left academics, and some in the media. It is a totally phony charge concocted as part of Hamas's strategy—supported by many on the hard left—to delegitimate and demonize the Jewish state. Israel is the only democracy in the world ever accused of war crimes when it fights a defensive war to protect its civilians. This is remarkable, especially in light of the fact that Israel has killed far fewer civilians than any other country in the world that has faced comparable threats. This, despite the fact that no one can now deny that Hamas had employed a deliberate policy of using children, schools, mosques, apartment buildings, and other civilian areas as shields from behind which to launch its deadly anti-personnel rockets. The Israeli Air Force has produced unchallengeable video evidence of this Hamas war crime.

Just to take one comparison, consider the wars waged by Russia against Chechnya and Ukraine. In these wars Russian troops have killed tens of thousands of Chechnyan and Ukrainian civilians, some of them willfully, at close range and in cold blood. Yet those radical academics who scream bloody murder against Israel rarely call for war crime tribunals to be convened against Russia. Nor have they called for war crime charges to be filed against any other of the many countries that routinely kill civilians, not in an effort to stop enemy terrorists, but just because it is part of their policy.

Nor did we see the Nazi-type rallies that were directed against Israel when hundreds of thousands of civilians were being murdered in Rwanda, in Darfur, and in other parts of the world. These bigoted hatefests are reserved for Israel.

The accusation of war crimes is nothing more than a tactic selectively invoked by Israel's enemies. Those who cry "war crime" against Israel don't generally care about war crimes, as such. Indeed, they often support them when engaged in by countries they like. What these people care about, and all they seem to care about, is Israel. Whatever Israel does is wrong regardless of the fact that so many other countries do worse.

When I raised this concern in a debate, my opponent accused me of changing the subject. He said we are talking about Israel now, not Chechnya or Darfur. This reminded me of a famous exchange between Harvard's racist president, Abbott Lawrence Lowell, and the great American judge Learned Hand. Lowell announced that he wanted to reduce the number of Jews at Harvard, because "Jews cheat." Judge Hand replied that "Christians also cheat." Lowell responded, "You're changing the subject. We are talking about Jews."

Well, you can't just talk about Jews. Nor can you just talk about Israel. Any discussion of war crimes must be comparative and contextual. If Russia did not commit war crimes when its soldier's massacred tens of thousands of Chechens and Ukrainians (not even in a defensive wars) then on what basis could Israel be accused of accidentally killing a far fewer number of human shields in an effort to protect its civilians? What are the standards? Why are they not being applied equally? Can human rights endure in the face of unequal and selective applications? These are the questions the international community should be debating, not whether Israel, and Israel alone, violated the norms of that vaguest of notions called "international law" or the "law of war."

If Israel, and Israel alone among democracies fighting defensive wars, were ever to be charged with "war crimes," that would mark the end of international human rights law as a neutral arbitrator of conduct. Any international tribunal that was to charge Israel, having not charged the many nations that have done far worse, will lose any remaining legitimacy among fair-minded people of good will.

If the laws of war in particular, and international human rights in general, are to endure, they must be applied to nations in order of the seriousness of the violations, not in order of the political unpopularity of the nations. If the law of war were applied in this manner, Israel would be among the last, and certainly not the first, charged.

Israel's actions in Gaza are justified under international law, and Israel should be commended for its self-defense against terrorism. Article 51 of the United Nations Charter reserves to every nation the right to engage in self-defense against armed attacks.

The residents of Sderot—who have borne the brunt of the attacks—have approximately fifteen seconds from launch time to run into a shelter. Although deliberately targeting civilians is a war crime, terrorists firing at Sderot are so proud of their actions that they sign their weapons.

When Barack Obama visited Sderot and saw the remnants of these rockets, he reacted by saying that if his two daughters were exposed to rocket attacks in their home, he would do everything in his power to stop such attacks. He understood how the terrorists exploit the morality of democracies.

In an incident related to me by the former head of the Israeli air force, Israeli intelligence learned that a family's house in Gaza was being used to manufacture rockets. The Israeli military gave the residents thirty minutes to leave. Instead, the owner called Hamas, which sent mothers carrying babies to the house.

Hamas knew that Israel would never knowingly fire at a home with civilians in it. They also knew that if Israeli authorities did not learn there were civilians in the house and fired on it, Hamas would win a public relations victory by displaying the dead. Israel held its fire. The Hamas rockets that were protected by the human shields were then used against Israeli civilians.

These despicable tactics—targeting Israeli civilians while hiding behind Palestinian civilians—can only work against moral democracies that care deeply about minimizing civilian casualties.

The Hamas tactic would not have worked against the Russians in Chechnya. When the Russians were fired upon, they fired against civilians without hesitation, killing thousands (with little international protest). Nor would it have worked in Darfur, where Janjaweed militias killed thousands of civilians and displaced 2.5 million in order to get the rebels who were hiding among them. Certain tactics work only against moral enemies who care deeply about minimizing civilian casualties.

The claim that Israel has violated the principle of proportionality—by killing more Hamas terrorists than the number of Israeli civilians killed by Hamas—is absurd. First, there is no legal equivalence between the deliberate killing of innocent civilians and the deliberate killings of Hamas combatants. Under the laws of war, any number of combatants can be killed to prevent the killing of even one innocent civilian.

Second, proportionality is not measured by the number of civilians actually killed, but rather by the relationship between the military value of the target and the number of enemy civilians who would be put at risk by destroying that target. When a military target is of high value—such as the headquarters of the enemy military or an area from which many rockets are being fired—the opposing military has more justification in risking collateral damage to enemy civilians.

While Israel installs warning systems and builds shelters, Hamas refuses to do so, precisely because it wants to maximize the number of Palestinian civilians inadvertently killed by Israel's military actions. Hamas knows from experience that even a small number of innocent Palestinian civilians killed inadvertently will result in bitter condemnation of Israel by many in the international community.

Israel understands this as well. It goes to enormous lengths to reduce the number of civilian casualties—even to the point of foregoing legitimate targets that are too close to civilians.

Until the world recognizes that Hamas is committing three war crimes—targeting Israeli civilians, using Palestinian civilians as human shields, and seeking the destruction of a member state of the United Nations—and that Israel is acting in self-defense and out of military necessity, the conflict will continue.

K. The Only Way to Deter Terrorist Attacks on Israel Is to Punish Who's Responsible—Iran

There are many losers in Hamas's war-crime attack against Israeli civilians. Primary among them are the Israeli women, children, and other civilians who have been killed, wounded, and kidnapped. They also include Israeli soldiers as well as Palestinian civilians who are forced to serve as human shields to protect Hamas terrorists. Hamas terrorists have also been killed, but they deserve no sympathy.

There can be no doubt about who instigated the attack. Hamas and Hezbollah are wholly-owned subsidiaries of the Iranian mullahs, who call the shots. Even if America cannot prove that Iran explicitly ordered the slaughter in Southern Israel, it is clearly responsible for the terror perpetrated by Hamas.

The only way to stop Hamas and Hezbollah terrorism is to punish Iran. No matter how much damage Israel inflicts on the Hamas military, Iran-inspired terrorism will not be deterred. Iran will continue to encourage Hamas to initiate new violence. This is especially so in light of the "success" of the recent massacres in achieving the goals of both Hamas and Iran: the murder of Israeli Jews with an eye to the destruction of Israel.

Regardless of what direct role Iran may or may not have played in orchestrating this massacre, it is indisputable that Iran has provided the military and financial support without which such massacres would not be possible. Even if American intelligence cannot prove that Iran explicitly ordered this action, it is clearly responsible for it and other atrocities perpetrated by Hamas and Hezbollah.

It is obvious that only Iran can permanently put an end to the recurring violence. And the only way to persuade Iran to terminate its role as the primary supporter of terrorism in the Middle East would be to punish the regime if it persists in facilitating such abominations: every act of Iran-inspired terrorism should be countered with punitive actions.

America is controlling $6 billion of Iranian funds. This money is supposed to be used for humanitarian purposes, but as the Iranian leadership has said, it will be used for whatever purposes Iran decides. Money is fungible, and the more Iran receives, the more of it can be sent to Hamas. This means more terrorism, more massacres, more kidnappings, more lynchings, and more rapes.

Even were the United States to permanently refreeze the funds—as it has temporarily done—and impose more severe economic sanctions, this would not deter Iran from inciting and ordering Hamas to commit more terror, because their zeal cannot be cooled by financial considerations.

Iran's primary goals are obvious: to prevent a deal between Saudi Arabia and Israel and to sow disarray throughout the region. The regime may well succeed, as it has thus far.

Another goal is to marginalize the Palestinian Authority and elevate Hamas, thus making a two-state solution impossible—because Hamas will not settle for anything less than Israel's total destruction. Israel has been trying to deter Hamas and Hezbollah for decades.

Not surprisingly, it's only worked sporadically.

Whenever Iran wants attacks against Israel to resume, Hamas and Hezbollah follow its orders. These terrorist groups are not deterrable because they are not the real decision makers. Only Iran can be deterred. But it is not being deterred because it's allowed to benefit when these attacks occur. Deterrence only works when the decision-makers themselves understand they will be severely hurt, not helped, if they take the actions we want deterred. The only way to stop Hamas's and Hezbollah's recurring attacks against Israel is to treat Iran as the attacker and punish it more than its puppet organizations.

This will not be easy to do, but there are several options, all of which require America's cooperation. Israel alone can hurt Iran but not enough to serve as a permanent deterrent.

Primary among the options is the destruction of Iran's nuclear-weapons program. If such an attack succeeded, it would be a win not only for Israel but for the entire region as well as for America and for peace. But the risks of such an attack are considerable, especially if Israel must do it alone. With the help of the United States, the military risks would be reduced. The successful destruction of Iran's nuclear program might weaken the government and could ultimately lead to regime change.

The bottom line is that unless Iran is severely punished for instigating terrorist attacks, these attacks will not be significantly deterred by Israeli military actions against the terrorist organizations. Such actions may slow the terrorists down by destroying their weapons and infrastructure, but it won't destroy their willingness to follow Iran's directives. And Iran will certainly send more weapons and materiel.

Recall as well that Hamas and Hezbollah members are religious fanatics who are not deterred by the risk of death. They welcome becoming martyrs. Iran, too, is run by religious fanatics, but they are *calculating* fanatics who would be deterred by credible threats to their nuclear program and regime. And many in the Iranian military, scientific, and technological areas are more secular than their leaders and capable of being deterred.

This attack Iran orchestrated may provide Israel and the United States their best justification for doing what they have long wanted to do: destroy Iran's nuclear-weapons program. Although the international community would publicly criticize such a military action, many world leaders, including in Saudi Arabia and other Arab states, would understand and even welcome it because they realize the world will be better off if the terrorist state of Iran does not have a nuclear arsenal.

One point is clear: Iran is a legitimate military target for Israel. Iran, through its surrogates, has waged war on Israel. Under international law, Israel has the right to retaliate militarily. It also has the right to take preemptive military action to prevent the mullahs from obtaining nuclear weapons they have threatened to use against Israel. A military attack on Iran's nuclear program would be justified both on retaliatory and preventive grounds.

Another option would be to persuade Saudi Arabia to recognize and normalize relationships with Israel. Since one of the apparent goals of the Iranian-backed Hamas massacres was to derail progress toward such an arrangement, it would send a powerful message to the Iranian leadership if the Hamas attack were to be seen as backfiring.

Another benefit of focusing on Iran, instead of exclusively on Hamas, might be to encourage Israel to exercise more restraint during its difficult incursion into Gaza. Israel, of course, has the right to do so, but such an extended incursion would be costly both in terms of Israeli lives and the lives of Palestinian human shields who are deliberately placed in harm's way by Hamas.

If Israel knew it could come out of this disaster with a weakened Iran, especially one without a nuclear weapons program, it might be willing to forgo its right to destroy Hamas.

Another hard step America could take would be to make new demands on Iran's and Hamas's most important ally in the region—namely Qatar. We could demand that Qatar extradite the Hamas leaders who are now hiding in plain view in Doha. We could demand that Qatar end its financial aid to Hamas, since these dollars, which are supposed to be used for humanitarian purposes, are in fact, used to support terrorism. We could demand that Qatar end or at least weaken its cozy relationship with Iran.

Qatar is playing a role in negotiations regarding the Israelis being held hostage by Hamas. That role can continue if it produces sufficient results.

To be sure, the United States has an important military base in Qatar, but it could be moved to Bahrain. This would be costly to both Qatar and to us, but it would send an important message of American strength.

Most importantly, America must continue its unconditional and hopefully bipartisan support for Israel's efforts to protect its own citizens and be in the forefront of the worldwide effort to fight terrorism.

L. Can the Whole World Be Wrong about Israel?

A British university student, having observed rabid demonstrations against Israel all over the world, once asked me a poignant question: Can the whole world be wrong when it condemns Israel? The answer is two-fold: First, it is not the whole world that is condemning Israel, though it is much of the world. Israel's actions, in defending itself against terrorists murdering its civilians, have been understood by most Americans, by many Canadians, by some Europeans, and by even a few Arabs. But it is true that the vast majority of people around the world engage in knee-jerk condemnation of Israel whenever it engages in self-defense—and even when it does nothing but exist. To the extent that most of the world engages in such automatic demonization of the Jewish state, the answer to the student's question is clear: Yes, when it comes to Israel, the world can be—and often is—wrong. Completely wrong. Immorally wrong. Sometimes anti-Semitically wrong.

This should come as no surprise to anyone familiar with Jewish history: for more than a thousand years, the whole world—at least the whole Christian world—believed that Jews ritually murdered Christian children to get their blood for use in the making of Passover matzoh. Now, much of the Arab and Muslim world still believe the blood libel. But regardless of how widespread these anti-Semitic views may be, they are simply as wrong as the widespread view, through most of human history, that the sun revolves around the earth, that the universe is six thousand years old, or that Israel deliberately bombed the Gaza hospital.

So is the view that Israel is at fault in the actions it is taking in Gaza after years of allowing Hamas rockets to play Russian roulette with the lives of its children, and now slaughtering children and adults alike. Right and wrong—whether factual or moral—are not determined by public opinion polls. In 2003, a European Commission survey found that 59 percent of Europeans regarded Israel as the greatest threat to world peace, ahead of rogue states like Iran and North Korea.[10] And a study conducted by the Anti-Defamation League in late 2008 and early 2009 revealed that 31 percent of Europeans blamed Jews for the global financial and economic crisis.[11] These polls results tell us more about Europe than about Israel, or Jews. More recent polls show an increase in these and other anti-Semitic views.

The pervasive ignorance among many European and American students regarding basic facts—for example, who started the 1948, 1967, and 1973 wars? What were the Palestinians offered by the Clinton-Barak proposals of 2000–01 and the Ehud Olmert proposal of 2008? When did the rocket attacks against Israeli civilians begin?—is staggering.

There is also much willful blindness regarding the facts and figures of the various Gaza wars. Hamas puts out false information and exaggerated figures that are immediately accepted by much of the media and many human rights groups. Evidence of such distortion was, according to a report in the *Jerusalem Post* provided by Col.

---

10 European Commission, "Iraq and Peace in the World," Flash Eurobarometer survey, November 2003, http://europa.eu.int/comm/public_opinion/flash/fl151 _iraq_full_report.pdf.

11 Anti-Defamation League, "ADL Survey in Seven European Countries Finds Anti-Semitic Attitudes Steady; 31 Percent Blame Jews for Financial Crisis," Press Release, February 10, 2009, http://www.adl.org/PresRele/ASInt_13/5465_13.htm.

Moshe Levi, the head of the IDF's Gaza Coordination and Liaison Administration (CLA), which compiled the IDF figures. As an example of such distortion, he cited the incident near a UN school in Jabalya in which initial Palestinian reports falsely claimed IDF shells had hit the school and killed forty or more people, many of them civilians.

In fact, he said, twelve Palestinians were killed in the incident— nine Hamas operatives and three noncombatants. Furthermore, as had since been acknowledged by the UN, the IDF was returning fire after coming under attack, and its shells did not hit the school compound.

"From the beginning, Hamas claimed that forty-two people were killed, but we could see from our surveillance that only a few stretchers were brought in to evacuate people," said Levi, adding that the CLA contacted the PA Health Ministry and asked for the names of the dead. "We were told that Hamas was hiding the number of dead."

As a consequence of the false information, he added, the IDF was setting up a "response team" for future conflicts whose job would be to collect information, analyze it and issue reports as rapidly as possible that refuted Hamas fabrications.

The IDF has now also identified hundreds of combatants who were killed in the fighting and estimates that most of the unidentified bodies yet to be identified were those of "terror operatives." Many others, who were classified as noncombatants, were human shields such as wives and children of Hamas military commanders who refused to allow their families to leave his home even after they were warned by Israel that their homes would be bombed.[12] The same is true today.

Ignorance is the father and mother of bigotry. It is also its child. Because emotion based on prejudice rather than reason based on information often drives the reaction to Israel, many anti-Israel agitators deliberately dumb it down, substituting slogans for facts, chanting for thinking and bigotry for fairness. Not surprisingly, much of this occurs on university campuses, orchestrated by hard-left

---

12 See *Jerusalem Post*. February 15, 2009.

professors who see their mission as propagandizing for the most radical elements of the Palestinian movement, rather than as teaching critical thinking or conveying unbiased information. Many of
these rabidly anti-Israel polemicists are Jewish—at least on their parent's side. Some are Israelis—or Israeli expatriates living in Europe
or America. They use their Jewish heritage or Israeli citizenship as
phony credibility chips. In effect, they offer an opposite, but equally
irrational, version of the argument *ad hominem*: "Consider our arguments not on their merits or demerits, but on the basis of who is
offering them." Or put more bluntly: "We are Jews—or Israelis. If
even we demonize Israel, it must indeed be demonic."

Constructive criticism of Israel and its policies is healthy. It is
ongoing in Israel and among its supporters throughout the world.
Demonizing the Jewish state or subjecting its actions to a double
standard is wrong and must be answered in the marketplace of ideas.
That is why I wrote and published the material in this short book.
I will continue to fight against those who would destroy Israel—by
mass murder, rockets, suicide bombs, nuclear weapons, falsehoods,
bigotry, divestments, boycotts, or any other means—as long as I have
the strength to do so.

M. A Modern-Day Blood Libel

On the wall of my office hangs a document from the end of the fif-
teenth century. It features an illustration of a bearded Jew extract-
ing the blood of a Christian child. The adjoining text explains that
Jewish law requires that Passover matzoh be baked with the blood of
Christian children.

These libelous documents were widely circulated through Europe
during the Easter season and led to frequent pogroms—murder, rape,
and destruction—against Jewish children, women, and men in
revenge for the alleged bleeding of Christian children.

There was never any actual evidence of such bleeding. In fact,
Jewish law explicitly prohibits the consumption of blood or its use in
cooking (that's why kosher steaks are so dry!).

But the evidence and lack thereof didn't matter to those who
were taught and believed what has come to be known as "the blood

libel." That falsehood was "true" despite all the evidence to the contrary. The blood libel persisted throughout Europe into the early twentieth century. Jews were put on trial, executed, and lynched for allegedly bleeding and killing Christian children.

Other libels against Jews formed the basis for classic anti-Semitism culminating in the Nazi lies that dehumanized Jews to an extent that made the Holocaust possible. Flowing the murder of 6 million innocent Jewish babies and adults, the world said, "never again" and anti-Semitism abated in many parts of the world.

Now it is back with a vengeance, accompanied by blood libels and other systematic lies about the Jewish people and their nation state Israel.

It is against this sordid historical background that the current blood libel—that Israel targeted a Gaza hospital deliberately causing the death of seven hundred Muslim children, women, and men (later reduced by Hamas to 470—which American intelligence has concluded was way exaggerated)—can best be understood and assessed.

There is absolutely no evidence that Israel targeted the hospital in order to kill innocent Palestinian civilians. Yet, that blood libel is widely believed by Israel's enemies. The "Muslim Street" has been indoctrinated by their leaders to believe anything negative about Jews or Israel. And the Arab media generally reports Hamas lies and exaggerations—such as the original claim that seven hundred civilians were killed at the hospital—as unvarnished truth.

It is unlikely that all the facts surrounding the tragedy at the Gaza hospital will emerge. Much of the evidence is under the control of Hamas, which can suppress, manipulate, or manufacture. Credible intelligence agencies around the world have assessed the likelihood of various scenarios: an errant terrorist rocket; the residue of an iron dome defensive missile; a misfired Israeli rocket; a targeted Israeli rocket. The current consensus is that it was a terrorist rocket that misfired, as apparently 15 to 20 percent of such rockets do and land in Gaza. The remnants of the explosive device might help in proving whose rocket it was, but Hamas refuses to produce any fragments, falsely claiming they disintegrated upon impact. I am aware of no objective assessment that points the finger at an Israeli rocket, and I am certain that none have concluded that the evidence points to the deliberate targeting of the hospital with the intent to kill civilians.

Yet that is precisely the blood libel that Israel's enemies—in Gaza, on the Muslim Street, in the Arab media and on university campuses around the world—are fomenting.

The current reaction to the events in Gaza cannot be understood without taking into account the long history of blood libels and Jew hatred. The current focus is on Gaza, but the goal of Hamas supporters is what Hamas itself proclaims in its charter: the end any nation state for the Jewish people in any part of Israel. This is not about any occupation or settlements. The chants and slogans come right out of the Hamas charter: "Palestine will be free from the river to the sea." That means that the area between the Jordan River and the Mediterranean Sea must be judenrein—free of Jews.

Anti-Semitism has always been based on lies. No amount of evidence, regardless of how strong, can persuade fervent Jew haters to accept the truth.

In the weeks to come, Israeli rockets will accidentally kill Palestinian civilians, because Hamas deliberately uses its children, women, the elderly, and others as human shields. Some are willing shields; others are pressured or forced to risk their lives to protect Hamas killers. The international law of "proportionality" allows Israel to destroy important military targets—such as Hamas leaders or rocket launchers—even they know that a certain number of civilians may be killed or injured. The only requirement is that the military value of the target be proportional to the number of anticipated collateral deaths and injuries among civilians. And the rule of proportionality also depends on how "civilian" these "civilians" actually are. Israel has more leeway in endangering the lives of civilians who volunteer to be shields, or who are in other ways complicit with Hamas, than they would be with regard to young children or others who are completely innocent.

But don't expect the blood libeling liars of Hamas or their cheerleaders to consider these and other legal and moral distinctions. For them every death of a Palestinian is automatically the fault of Israel, even if they are killed by an errant terrorist rocket, or while being used by Hamas as a human shield. The truth simply doesn't matter to bigots who perpetuate blood libels.

N. How to Assure That Terrorist Attacks against Israeli Civilians Will Recur

There is one sure fire way of guaranteeing that Hamas will continue to employ terrorism against Israel and that other terrorist groups will increase the use of terrorism against civilians around the world. That sure fire way is to reward the terrorists who employ this tactic and to punish their intended victims who try to fight back. This is one of the most important lessons to be learned from the recent events in Gaza, but it is not a new lesson. In 2002, I wrote a book entitled *Why Terrorism Works*. The point I made in that book is even more relevant today than it was then:

> The real root cause of terrorism is that it is successful—terrorists have consistently benefited from their terrorist acts. Terrorism will persist as long as it continues to work for those who use it, as long as the international community rewards it, as it has been doing for the past thirty-five years.

Hamas has been greatly rewarded by the international community, by human rights groups, by the media, by many students and professors, as well as by millions of decent people, despite Hamas's indecent multiple war crimes of butchering civilians, firing rockets at Israeli civilians and hiding behind Palestinian human shields. And Israel has been significantly punished for trying to protect its citizens from these attacks. Although Hamas will almost certainly suffer significant military defeat at the hands of the IDF, it has gained a public relations bonanza. Its status in academia and in many parts of the world has been enhanced, as it has at the United Nations and throughout the Arab street. It will lose the battle on the ground in Gaza but may have won the war in the hearts and minds of many decent, and many more indecent, people throughout the world.

So here, in simple terms, is the twelve-step program that the international community should follow if it truly wants to see terrorism become the primary tactic used against democracies by those with perceived grievances.

Step 1: Use terrorism—murderous rampages, rockets aimed at civilians, suicide bombings in pizza parlors and discothèques, bombs planted in school buses, shootings in classrooms, etc.—as widely as possible against your enemies, to the point where they have no option but to respond militarily.

Step 2: Make sure that the terrorists and their weapons—rockets, explosives, etc.—are hidden among civilians in densely populated areas.

Step 3: When the inevitable responses occur, employ human shields, the younger the better. Recruit them voluntarily, if possible, but commandeer them, if necessary, even if they're babies or toddlers.

Step 4: Be certain that your terrorist fighters are wearing civilian clothing. Recruit as many women and teenage youngsters as possible to become terrorists.

Step 5: Be ready with video cameras and sympathetic journalists to videotape every single death and transmit them as widely as possible to media outlets around the world.

Step 6: Recycle dead civilians, especially children, and move them from media to media, thus multiplying the number of apparently dead civilians.

Step 7: Be certain that sympathetic doctors and United Nations personnel overstate the number of civilians killed, counting every person under the age of eighteen and every woman as a civilian, even if they are terrorists.

Step 8: Circulate totally false reports about civilian casualties and their location by, for example, claiming that more than seven hundred civilians were killed in the Gaza hospital when far fewer were killed in the parking lot. You can be confident that the media will put your exaggerated reports on the front page, and when the truth eventually comes out, after careful investigation days or weeks later, it will be buried in the back pages.

Step 9: Accuse the democracy of war crimes and bring cases against its leaders and soldiers in courts sympathetic to Hamas around the world. Bringing the lawsuits will create a presumption of guilt, even if the charges are dismissed months or years later.

Step 10: Schedule various United Nations "debates" at which tyrannical dictatorships from around the world line up at the podium to condemn Israel for crimes routinely committed by these dictatorships but not by Israel.

Step 11: Trot out the usual stable of reliable anti-Israel academics to flood newspapers and television shows with some of the worst drivel about international law, human rights, and the laws of war—drivel that would earn students' failing grades in any objective law school course on these subjects. Organize one-sided protests by students and other young people around the world.

Step 12: Make sure that Hamas understands that if it repeats its multiple war crime strategy, it will once again be rewarded, and if Israel fights back, it will once again be punished.

These twelve steps are for use by university students, nations, and organizations, such as the United Nations, which seem determined to encourage terrorism.

Now here are six steps for those democracies that would actually like to put an end to terrorist attacks against its civilians.

Step 1: Never, under any circumstances, reward an act of terrorism or a group that employs terrorism to achieve its goals.

Step 2: Always punish terrorists and terrorist groups that employ, facilitate, or support terrorism against civilians. Also punish nations that fund and support them.

Step 3: Never punish democracies that seek to prevent acts of terrorism against their civilians, especially when the terrorists hide among their own civilians in order to provoke democracies into killing civilians.

Step 4: Never allow human rights, international organizations, or war crime tribunals to be hijacked by the supporters of terrorism and the enemies of democracy to punish only those who seek to protect their civilians against terrorism. This is especially true when the democracies have been patient in responding and have no reasonable alternative course other than military self-defense.

Step 5: Never manipulate the emotions of decent people by showing only the human shields who have been killed by military self-defense actions of the democracies, without explaining that it was the terrorists who caused these deaths.

Step 6: Make certain that the cause espoused by the terrorists is set back by every act of terrorism.

As I wrote in 2002:

> Not only must terrorism never be rewarded, the cause of those who employ it must be made—and must be seen to be made—worse off as a result of the terrorism than it would have been without it. The manner by which calculating terrorists define and calibrate the cost and benefits may be different from the way common criminals decide whether to rob, cheat, or bully, but society's response must be based on similar considerations. Those who employ terrorism have their own criteria for evaluating success and failure, and in implementing the immutable principle that those who employ terrorism must be worse off for having resorted to this tactic, we must make them worse off by their own criteria.

The international community, by and large, has been doing the opposite. The message it has been sending has been: keep it up. It will only help your terrorist cause and hurt your democratic enemy. No wonder Hamas, and other terrorist's groups, regard their war crimes tactic as a win-win for terrorism and a lose-lose for democracy.

O. Myths about Gaza Must Be Corrected

Hamas's strongest weapon in its war of words against Israel is the big lie. Hamas has put forth a series of untruths, many of which have been parroted by members of the media, student protestors and even government officials. Some go back to the founding of Israel seventy-five years ago, others are in today's headlines.

Consider first the blood libel that Israel was responsible for the bombing of a Gaza hospital in which seven hundred civilians were murdered. That narrative is believed throughout the Arab and Muslim world, and in many parts of the rest of the world, especially among student radicals. The evidence to the contrary is overwhelming: virtually every intelligence agency has concluded that Israel did not fire the deadly rocket and it almost certainly came from Islamic Jihad, and that the number of dead—including terrorists and accomplices—is on the lower side of between one hundred and three hundred, not the inflated figures put out by Hamas.

A related lie is that Israel deliberately targets civilian areas in what is the densest part of the world. The truth, of course, is that Gaza is relatively dense in population, but nowhere close to other major cities such as Tel Aviv, Manhattan, Manila, and other Asian metropolises. According to one study, it ranks sixty-third in density. I have been in Gaza and have seen the open fields from which Hamas could easily fire its rockets if it didn't want to endanger its own civilians. But as leaders of Hamas have publicly admitted, they deliberately fire from schools, mosques, hospitals, and other areas where they know civilians will be when Israel justifiably seeks to destroy the rocket launches.

This is part of their game plan: to attack Israeli civilians, requiring Israel to respond, and expecting that Israel will cause collateral damage to the Palestinian human shields, whose bodies can then be paraded in front of willing media cameras. This has been the pattern for more than a quarter of a century.

The other myth is that Hamas is an open-air prison and that its prison guards are Israelis. The truth is that Israel removed every single civilian and soldier (including bodies of their dead that had been buried for years) when Israel ended its occupation in 2005. Israel left behind farm implements, hot houses and other facilities that could have been used to help the people of Gaza. European countries donated money in the effort to turn the Gaza Strip into Singapore on the Mediterranean. But after Hamas defeated the Palestinian

Authority in the legislative elections, Hamas terrorists conducted a coup and killed and exiled members of the Palestinian executive, who had also been duly elected. As soon as Hamas took total control of the Gaza Strip, it turned Gaza into a hellhole of poverty and lack of freedoms, including religion, speech, and education. Gaza is not an open-air prison, but what it is has been the result exclusively of the actions of Hamas.

As soon as Hamas was able to, it began to use Gaza city as a launching pad for thousands of rockets endangering the lives of Israeli citizens. It was as a response to these attacks that Israel imposed limits on Palestinian exists and entries to the Gaza Strip.

Notwithstanding these limits, thousands of Palestinians were permitted to come into Israel on a daily basis to work and earn much higher salaries than they could have gotten in Gaza. It now turns out that some of these guest-workers were Hamas spies who provided the terrorists with information that was used to slaughter fourteen hundred Israelis and others on October 7.

The other current myth is that it is Israel that is causing the humanitarian crisis in Gaza by denying it fuel and other necessities. The truth is that Hamas has stores of fuel, water, medicine, and food in the tunnels to which ordinary Palestinians are denied entry. These protective tunnels and humanitarian items are reserved exclusively for Hamas fighters. Hamas can help prevent the humanitarian crisis by giving its supply of fuel to hospitals, instead of using them for the rockets they fire into Israel. Hamas leaders have stolen billions of dollars that were intended to provide humanitarian aid to Palestinian civilians.

The greatest enemy of the Palestinian people is not Israel, it is Hamas. Israel would be doing the Palestinian people a great favor if it can eliminate Hamas, just as it would be doing a great favor to the Lebanese people if it could eliminate Hezbollah. Iran is the puppet master behind both of these terrorist groups and supports their war against the Palestinian and Lebanese people who want to live in peace with Israel.

Recently, the secretary general of the United Nations, who has generally been less anti-Israel than some of his predecessors, made an outrageous statement seeking to put into "context" the beheadings, rapes, murders, and kidnappings of fourteen hundred innocent people. Putting such barbarity in context can only be seen as an attempt to justify it, or at least excuse it. Making such a statement disqualifies the head of the United Nations from playing any constructive role in the current crisis. He has become part of the problem, rather than part of the solution. There is no excuse for justification for what Hamas did, or for what so many student and other groups around the world have sought to justify.

Hamas's barbarity has put Israel into a difficult situation: it must respond by destroying Hamas, but it cannot destroy Hamas without endangering the lives of the human shields that have become Hamas's primary defense against Israeli counter attacks. Striking the appropriate balance is always difficult—especially with kidnapped Israelis also being used as shields—but the world must understand that every Palestinian or Israeli civilian who dies as the result of the Hamas attacks and its use of civilians as human shields is entirely the fault of Hamas—legally, politically, and morally.

Consider the following analogous case: A bank robber takes a hostage and begins shooting customers from behind his hostage shield. In an effort to stop the shooting, a bank guard takes aim at the shooter but accidentally kill the hostage. Every legal system holds the hostage taker guilty of murdering the shield, not the guard whose bullet actually killed him. The same should be true of Hamas.

Unless and until the world recognizes and acts on this reality, the Hamas tactic will continue, and more and more civilians—both Israelis and Palestinians—will die.

P. There Are No "Pro-Palestinian" Rallies

Despite the media headlines about pro-Palestinian rallies and protests on university campuses, cities around the world and the Arab street, the reality is that there has not been a single rally that is actually pro-Palestinian. All of them have been anti-Israel, pro-Hamas, pro-terrorism and often anti-Semitic. None have called for a two-state solution. Instead, they have chanted about eliminating Jews "from the river to the sea"—which is all of Israel.

The most anti-Palestinian entity in the world is Hamas. They have killed and exiled elected officials from the Palestinian Authority. They have stolen food, fuel, money, and medical supplies from the Palestinian people. They have used Palestinian children and women as human shields. They have prevented Gaza's civilians from moving south and away from Israeli bombing. They have denied Gazans the right to education and to religious and political freedom. They have made life miserable for their people. They have caused the deaths of more Palestinians than Israel has.

All this was well before the recent war with Israel started by the Hamas massacres, which Hamas knew would make things worse for the civilians of Gaza. Indeed, that was part of their motive in attacking Israel: to force Israel to respond forcefully so that the world would see dead Palestinian babies who they use as human shields.

Now things have gotten much worse and are likely to get even more serious in the future, as Hamas hoards the remaining fuel and humanitarian supplies This is all the fault of Hamas and its puppet master Iran.

It is anything but "pro-Palestinian" to support the anti-Palestinian policies of Hamas and its supporters. Yet the media persists in calling these viscous anti-Israel and anti-Jewish rallies "pro-Palestinian," which makes them seem more positive and acceptable to the general public.

The same is true of anti-Israel and pro-Hamas organizations such as "Students for Justice in Palestine." That organization is against justice for Palestinians. If they wanted justice for the Palestinian people, they would oppose Hamas. They seek injustice for Israel and Jews. They hide their true beliefs behind a title that is entirely misleading about its goals and means. The same is true of the misnamed anti-Semitic group that calls itself "Jewish Voice for Peace," which is not really Jewish and opposes peace. But by falsely calling itself "Jewish," it seeks enhanced credibility for its mendacious accusations against Israel.

The time has come for good people to understand that this is not a conflict between people who are pro-Palestinian and pro-Israel. Many of us are both. I support a peaceful Palestinian state living side by side with Israel. Most Israelis agree that the two-state solution is the best—or the least worst—possible outcome. We want a democratic, peaceful Palestinian state that cares about the welfare of its people. It is precisely this goal that Hamas sought to undercut when it sent its murders and rapists into Israel on October 7.

Hamas realized that Israel and Saudi Arabia were on the verge of making a peace that would have required Israel to limit its West Bank settlements and to move toward a two-state solution, which would have been good for Palestinians. Such a peace would have been a game changer. Also, it would have marginalized Hamas and other terrorist groups that oppose peace and any two-state solution that allows Israel to continue to exist.

The current dispute is between a nation that would love to live in peace with its neighbors, and gangs of terrorists who would like nothing more than to overthrow all governments in the Middle East and substitute Islamic Caliphates that marginalize women, murder gays, and suppress dissent.

So, I ask the media to do its job by accurately describing the protests and demonstrations on university campuses and streets around the world. Do not label them as "pro-Palestinian." Truth in reporting requires that you label them as anti-Israel and pro-Hamas.

This will deny students who join these protests and sign letters in support of their goals the excuse that many are now using, that they were not aware that these groups support what Hamas did on October 7, and that they demand the end of Israel. Anyone who joins these "pro-Palestine" protests or signs their petitions should be aware of what they are supporting: not the Palestinian people who seek peace, but Hamas terrorists who seek to destroy Israel and the Jewish people.

There can be no doubt that Hamas, in addition to seeking the destruction of Israel, is an anti-Semitic hate group. It also opposes the rights of women, gays, transgender people, as well as freedom of speech and religion. These are all policies that progressives and wokes claim to support. Accordingly, the best proof that those who join the Hamas rallies and sign their petitions are complicit in anti-Semitism is that they are willing to support a group that opposes virtually all of their core values, as long as they also oppose Jews and their nation state.

Freedom of speech requires transparency and honesty. The media, by describing these bigoted groups as "pro-Palestine" while hiding their true agenda, disserves these important interests.

Q. Counting Deaths in Gaza

Hamas puts out claimed death tolls among Palestinians in three categories: total, children, and women. Our government disputes the figures, and for good reason, since Hamas has a long history of lying about casualties. But even if their figures were accurate, they hide the relevant truth: how many if the dead are active Hamas terrorists? How many are directly complicit in terrorism? How many are vocal supporters of Hamas terrorism? How many fourteen-, fifteen-, sixteen- and seventeen-year-olds who Hamas counts as "children" are combatants—child soldiers recrutied by Hamas—or accessories? How many women are Hamas terrorists or accessories?

How many were killed by misfiring terrorist rockets, as in the hospital parking lot? How many of those killed by Israeli fire are really totally innocent civilians, such as the very young children whose bodies Hamas eagerly displays on television? What are the actual percentages?

There is often no sharp line between combatants and civilians when it comes to Hamas terrorists and their facilitators, since Hamas does not have a regular army with uniforms and other criteria for distinguishing between the two. It is a continuum, with young children at the civilian end and complicit "civilians" at the combatant end, with many categories somewhere along the spectrum.

Hamas medical data deliberately denies the public the information necessary to honestly determine who and how many are closest to the civilian as compared to the combatant end.

Recall the Hamas videos showing bloodthirsty crowds chanting "Allahu Al Akbar" as bleeding Israeli women were driven and displayed through the streets possibly after being raped? Most of the cheering "civilians" in those crowds may be civilians as a matter of the law of war, but do they deserve the same sympathy as the dead babies that Hamas eagerly poses in front of TV cameras? No, it is a matter of degree.

What about members of the Hamas political wing? Where are they on the continuum? What about those who build, operate, or service the Hamas terror tunnels?

A common mantra is that Israel is at war only with Hamas, not with the Palestinian people of Gaza. That blinks the reality that many if not most of the Palestinian people of Gaza support the brutal tactics of Hamas. Even their young children are taught that killing Jews is good. This doesn't make the children complicit, but what about the teachers? Evan if it doesn't make them combatants, it surely makes them less sympathetic victims, especially if they follow Hamas orders not to try to move away from areas of combat.

Israel is at war with Hamas which controls Gaza politically and militarily. It is comparable to when America was at war with Germany and Japan in the 1940s. Civilians pay a price when their country attacks another country, as Hamas attacked Israel. Even when it is only a group within a country, such as Al Qaeda or ISIS, civilians die, as many did in Afghanistan and Iraq when the United States battled terrorists thousands of miles away from our homeland. Israel is fighting mass murderers just across its borders.

The result is many grey areas, as a matter of law and morality, which cannot be quantified by the simplistic tripartite categories that Hamas releases to the public, even if they were grossly accurate.

The overlaps among these and other categories are real and relevant. Every genuine civilian and young child that is killed is a tragedy, but these tragedies are entirely the fault and respon-sibility of Hamas. When Hamas decided to invade Israel and murder and rape its civilians, it knew that Israel would have to respond militarily and that Palestinian civilians would inevitably become collateral victims. Not only did Hamas know its attack would cause the death of Palestinians, it intended and desired that result as part of its "dead baby" play book. Hamas knows that

Israel never deliberately targets innocent babies. Why would it? It loses every time a dead Palestinian is displayed to TV cameras, as it is losing now in public opinion. Hamas also knows that despite every effort to avoid and reduce civilian casualties, some will occur, especially because Hamas uses them as human shields to protect its terrorists.

This tactic is well illustrated by the famous cartoon showing an Israeli soldier shooting from in front of a baby carriage to protect the baby, while a Hamas terrorist fires from behind a carriage, using the baby to protect him.

So, when you hear the number of Palestinians that Hamas claims were killed, ask hard questions. The number of totally innocent civilians may be far lower than the misleading totals released by Hamas partisans as parts of its public relations war against Israel.

R. Gays for Gaza, Jews for Hamas, Feminists for Terrorists, and Progressives for Fascists

Among the groups that have supported the rapes, beheadings mass murders and kidnappings of Jews by Hamas have been some that purport to speak for gays, Jews, feminists, and progressives. If any of these groups were actually to travel to Gaza, they would be murdered by Hamas, which has no tolerance for gays, Jews, feminists, or progressives. Indeed, among the people beheaded, raped, murdered, and kidnapped were gays, Jews who support Palestinians, feminists, and progressives. None of that matters to Hamas. If you are a Jew or an Israeli, you are a target of their barbarity.

Why do so many people from groups that Hamas seeks to destroy support that racist organization? The answer is clear: these bigots hate Jews and their nation state more than they like themselves and their groups. This has little to do with support for the Palestinian people who are horribly oppressed by Hamas. Nor does it reflect support for stateless, oppressed, or occupied national groups in general. These selective bigots are silent about the stateless Kurds, the oppressed Uighurs, and other groups that deserve their support. They only focus on the Palestinians because they are allegedly oppressed by the Jews.It is hatred of Jews, not love of the Palestinians or other groups that motivates these bigots.

Let us remember that these shows of support for Hamas began before Israel even responded to the Hamas barbarity. They were shows of support for what Hamas did to innocent Jews: rapes, beheadings, mass murders, and kidnapping. It was the victimization of Jews that stimulated these displays of anti-Semitism. There were few criticisms of Hamas for what it did. The most ferocious demonization was against Israel for what it is: the nation state of the Jewish people. And as is typical of bullies, it came when Israel was at its weakest and most vulnerable, still grieving the loss of so many innocent civilians.

Among the most hypocritical supporters of Hamas are Gays for Gaza. Rainbow flags and posters identifying the protesters as gay were rampant at anti-Israel demonstrations calling for the end of that nation. These signs are illegal in Gaza. Anyone displaying them would be killed, as former terrorist leader Mahmud Eshtawi, who was caught having sex with another man, was killed after being tortured.

Gay men in Gaza seek asylum in Israel, which is among the nation's most accepting of gays in the world. But none of this matters to the gay bigots who put their hatred of Jews above their concern for gay Palestinians.

Even worse is the misnamed group Jewish Voice for Peace, which has long served as a front for Hamas and other anti-Israel terrorist groups. It claims to be anti-Zionist, opposing the existence of Israel, but many of its leaders and supporters are overtly anti-Semitic. Its Facebook post recently featured such classic anti-Semitic tropes as: "Nazi Germany was a victim of the Jews;" Israelis are "the synagogue of Satan;" "we should erase Israel from the world map;" and "Israel was responsible for 9/11."

If its Jewish members (many members are not Jews despite its name) sought to protest in Gaza, they would be killed or kidnapped. Hamas, like the Nazis, doesn't distinguish among Jews based on their politics, as evidenced by the fact that some of the Jews killed on October 7 were critical of the Israeli government and perhaps even of Zionism. But that didn't matter to the rapists and beheaders of Hamas. To them a Jew is a Jew, regardless of whether they belong to Jewish Voice for Peace or Likud.

Then there are the feminists, progressives, and labor unions that support the Hamas brutality and oppose the existence of Israel.

Hamas is the among the most anti-feminist group in the world, subjugating women to the whims of their husbands and fathers and tolerating if not encouraging honor killing of women who dishonor their men.

Hamas imprisons progressive critics, and they do not permit independent labor unions. They exploit workers, using child laborers and soldiers. But not a word of criticism from the bigots who are willing to give them a pass on their fascism as long as they murder Jews. If this isn't anti-Semitism, I don't know what is.

Yes, Jews can be anti-Semites. So can gays, feminists, progressives, socialists, and others on the hard left. Hitler was a vegetarian. Some leading Nazis were gay. Gertrude Stein, a Nazi collaborator, was a Jew. Many university students and faculty not only in Germany but at Harvard, Yale, and Georgetown supported Nazi Germany in the 1930s. Today's Nazis are Hamas. Today's enablers of Nazism are the students and others who support Hamas. History will judge them the way history has judged Nazi collaborators.

S. The New Kristallnacht: The Widespread Praise for the Hamas Barbarism Shows the Breadth of Jew Hatred

Many of the most egregious petitions and protests against Israel occurred even before Israel responded to the Hamas barbarity of October 7. Student groups, lawyer groups, Black Lives Matter groups, labor unions, and other hard-left woke progressives praised Hamas for its rapes, beheadings, and murders just hours after they occurred. It would be as if these groups increased their support for Nazism following Kristallnacht in 1938, when several hundred Jews were killed in Germany.

The actual mass murders of October 7, bad as they were, are not the new Kristallnacht. It is the widespread reaction to these murders that, like Kristallnacht, demonstrates the depths of Jewish hatred and signals that the worse may be yet to come.

Now that Israel has begun its justified military response to the war declared by Hamas, matters have gotten even worse. But we must never forget how bad they already were before Israel fired a single shot. Throughout the world, Israel was blamed by bigots for causing the deaths, beheadings, and rapes of its own people. There used to be an expression in pre–second World War Poland, that "if something is wrong, the Jews must be behind it." Modern-day anti-Semites apply that finger pointing even to the victimization of Jews themselves: if Hamas murders Jews, it must be the fault of the nation state of the Jewish people. Now that Israel is defending its citizens against terrorists who use human shields, the blame-the-Jews mantra has gotten even more extreme.

The bottom line is Hamas is winning the information war even as it loses the war on the ground. Hamas leaders must be thinking that the mass murders of October 7 were a great success. They have generated anti-Israel resolutions by the United Nations, by university professors, by labor unions, and by many other organizations. Terrorism works. Barbarism succeeds. Rapes are rewarded. Beheadings are accepted. As long as the victims are Jews who brought it on themselves!

Columbia students and professors have deemed the Hamas war crimes to be appropriate "military" actions, justified by the occupation of the Gaza Strip that ended in 2005. The National Lawyers Guild refused to condemn Hamas. Nor has the United Nations and other international bodies. Hamas is being deemed the "victim" of Israeli crimes.

The "success" of the murderous rampage of October 7 will inevitably encourage other such "successes" in the future, since a success tends to be emulated, not only by the group that achieved it, but by others as well. So, if the international community and anti-Israel protesters continue to deliver a message of success to Hamas, their brutal tactics will be coming to a theatre near you.

For years I have been arguing that the root cause of terrorism is that it works! It is rewarded rather than punished. The reaction to the Hamas barbarism of October 7 is just another example of this tragic reality. But it adds a bizarre dimension. The more barbaric the terrorism, the more it seems to be rewarded. There has been support for Hamas following its worst instance of mass terrorism than there was before.

Such terrorism will only increase—in scope, intensity, and barbarity—if it continues to be rewarded as it is now.

I doubt that many of the ignorant, bigoted students who are marching and shouting in praise of Hamas understand that they will have blood on their hands when Hamas relies on their continuing support for more and bloodier terrorism. They should realize that they are on the wrong side of history, of morality, and of law. They are the modern-day version of the students in Munich and Berlin who started by burning books and ended by burning babies. Students have been on the forefront of some of the most horrible bloodbaths of history from Hitlerism to Stalinism to support for the ayatollahs. These bigoted ignoramuses may think they are different. So did their predecessors.

Kristallnacht was a wake-up call that too many, including too many Jews, slept through. The world, and especially the Jews, cannot afford to sleep through another wake-up call that is occurring right before our eyes.

T. Judging the Morality and Immorality of Pro-Hamas Protestors

Pro-Hamas protestors on university campuses and on streets around the world fall into several categories relevant to judging their morality and immorality. The most immoral are those like the thirty Harvard student organizations and the National Law Guild who expressly supported the Hamas rapes and beheadings even before Israel fired a single shot in response.

There is no moral or political justification for lending such support to rapists, beheaders, and kidnappers. Yet, these and other groups immediately showed their approval for Hamas barbarity, some claiming that it was an appropriate and entirely lawful military action. These groups and individuals have no claim to morality or decency.

The second-most immoral category consists of groups and individuals who were silent about the Hamas atrocities only after Israel began to engage in self-defense measures that caused collateral damage to civilians—that Hamas knew full well would result from its terrorist attack against Israel. By protesting only Israel, not Hamas, these groups and individuals also disqualified themselves from being taken seriously as moral agents.

Third are those groups and individuals who generally condemn Israel for its policies, without also condemning other nations whose policies are far more inconsistent with human rights. Primary among these groups are the United Nations and many individual countries that focus on Israel's imperfections to the exclusion of all other nations. Israel is the Jew among nations, and focusing only on the Jew is a form of international anti-Semitism.

A variation on the above is organizations such as Human Rights Watch which does address violations by groups other than Israel but focuses disproportionately on the nation state of the Jewish people. This double standard, too, is a form of international anti-Semitism.

The final category—and the one least deserving of moral criticism—are those individual and groups that focus on Israel and other countries in proportion to the seriousness of their violations. In theory, such groups have the highest claim to moral authority, but in practice, few such groups actually exist.

I am hard-pressed to think of a prominent organization, or even many prominent individuals, whose comparative criticism of Israel is proportionate to its comparative culpability. Even the United States government fails this test. Consider the well-intentioned criticism by the Obama administration against Israel for killing too many civilians in its legitimate effort to route out Hamas.

The United States itself killed many, many more innocent civilians in Iraq and Afghanistan when it was seeking, quite justifiably, to destroy ISIS and Al Qaeda. No one knows precisely how many civilians died as the result of American efforts to stop terrorist groups who were operating thousands of miles away from its borders, but the combined numbers are clearly in the hundreds of thousands.

These relatively recent deaths in Afghanistan and Iraq pale in comparison with the number of innocent civilians killed by the United States, Great Britain, and its allies in their just war against Nazism. Millions of Germans, Japanese, and enemy civilians were killed in the first bombings of Dresden, Tokyo, and other cities, and especially by the atomic bombs dropped on Hiroshima and Nagasaki.

The world understood that when nations attack other nations, the result will always be civilian deaths. Israel takes greater precautions than any country in the history of the world in trying to minimize civilian's deaths among Palestinians. Yet they are condemned for more than any other nation in history. This double standard, too, reflects bias and is relevant to judging the comparative morality of nations at war.

The First Amendment gives anti-Israel protestors the right to be immoral. It gives them the right to lie and to reflect anti-Semitic bigotry. But the First Amendment also gives us the right, indeed the responsibility, to call out this immorality, mendacity, and double standard.

So let the protests go forward. The best answer to immorality and double standards is not censorship, it is morality and truth. The marketplace of ideas must be open to all and should be as transparent as possible.

So, when you see an anti-Israel protest in the media, in the streets, or on college campuses, ask the hard questions: Who are these protestors? What is their agenda? What is their history? What are their biases? And do the protesters apply a single standard of morality?

The protesters are judging Israel. Let the world judge them as well.

U. Are Anti-Israel Protests Protected by the First Amendment?

The virulent anti-Israel protests on campuses and on the streets have once again raised the question of whether there are limits to freedom of speech. This age-old question recurs every time protests become dangerous and raise the possibility of violence.

The Supreme Court of the United States has tried hard over the last century to draw the line between protected speech and unprotected incitement to violence. Current law protects advocacy of violence, but not immediate incitement to violence. This line is anything but clear. As Oliver Wendell Holmes put it a century ago: "Every idea is an incitement." Yet the courts have tried—not always successfully—to distinguish between advocacy and incitement, without favoring some ideas over others. As the Supreme Court put it in 1990: "Under the First Amendment there is no such thing as a false idea. However pernicious an opinion may seem, we depend for its correction not on the conscience of judges and juries, but on the competition of other ideas."

Marxists can advocate legal overthrow of the government by force and violence as long as they do not immediately incite such violence. Hamas supporters can call for the end of Israel, but they can't incite an angry crowd to kill a specific Jew or Zionist. I had a case in the 1970s in which my client, a Stanford literature professor, spoke to a group of students, telling them it would be a good idea to take over the computation center which was helping the war effort in Vietnam. The students immediately followed the professor's admonition and unlawfully occupied the center, destroying parts of it. Stanford, being a private university, was not bound by the First Amendment, and so it fired the professor without directly addressing the question of whether his speech would have been protected by the First Amendment if Stanford had been a public university. Similarly difficult cases have resulted in different outcomes during the past thirty years.

The despicable and immoral pro-Hamas protests that are plaguing American universities today include some protected advocacy and some unprotected incitement, as well as some close questions. Because Hamas is a designated terrorist group, it is a crime to provide it with "material support," and courts have differed as to the meaning of "material." Verbal support alone is not enough, but collecting money for Hamas is. Harassment of an individual student—such as that which occurred at Harvard—is not protected, especially if it involves any physical contact or direct threats. Creating a "hostile environment" presents a difficult issue, since such an environment can be created by constitutionally protected speech.

One major problem on many of today's campuses is that anti-Israel and anti-Semitic speech cannot be disputed by "the competition of other ideas." Pro-Israel speakers, even those who advocate a Palestine state living in peace with Israel—as I do—are not invited to speak on many campuses. At the University of California Law School at Berkeley, several clubs have amended their rules to prohibit any Zionists to speak and present "other ideas" than ending Israel. The marketplace has been closed to pro-Israel advocacy. This selective censorship is not consistent with the First Amendment, but it is demanded in the false name of "Diversity, Equity and Inclusion (DEI)."

The DEI movement is against diversity of opinions, equality of ideas, and inclusion of Zionists and Jews. Its idea of free speech is "speech for me but not for thee." DEI has become the enemy of free speech, due process, and Jewish students. Yet its influence on many university campuses has grown dramatically, as DEI bureaucracies have taken over decision-making regarding campus speech and discipline.

Many progressive woke students, faculty, and administrators are opposed to free speech. They believe that speakers with views different from theirs should be shut down, as the Stanford Lawyers Guild shut down a conservative judge. But they demand an expansive definition of free speech for pro-Hamas demonstrators who harass, threaten, and create fear for many Jewish students. This double standard is unacceptable under any view of the First Amendment and the open marketplace of ideas, and no university should tolerate it.

V. Colleges That Tolerate Anti-Semitism Risk Lawsuits and Cutoff of Federal Funding

Hate speech and threats against Jewish students has become so rampant on many American campuses as to create a hostile and unsafe environment. University administrators face difficult challenges— legal, education, moral, and financial—in trying to deal with this growing concern.

Public universities are governed by the First Amendment, while private universities are free to censor constitutionally protected hate speech that violates its policies or its contracts with students. Some private universities claim to adhere to the spirit of the First Amendment even if not required to do so. Most do it selectively. But both public and private universities receive federal funding and are therefore bound by federal regulations that require them to create an atmosphere that is not hostile to religious or ethnic groups, even if that involves some limitations on protected hate speech.

Recently, Secretary of Education Miguel Cardona warned schools receiving such aid that if they are insensitive to anti-Semitism and Islamophobia on their campus, they could lose federal funding. At the same time, I and other lawyers have been called by numerous parents of Jewish students who are contemplating lawsuits against colleges to which they are paying tuition for their children. They report that Jewish students are experiencing hostile environments and threats to their safety. They point to events such as that which occurred at Harvard where a group of anti-Israel students surrounded a Jewish student, harassing him, blocking his exit, and reportedly knocking him to the ground. They also point to threats against Jewish fraternity houses, kosher kitchens, and other campus institutions frequented by Jewish students.

Although Secretary Cardona echoed the Biden administration in joining together anti-Semitism and Islamophobia as equal dangers on campus, it is obvious that the major hostilities today are directed at Jewish and Zionist students, rather than Islamic or Palestinian students. Indeed some, though not all, of the threats have come from Islamic and Arab students.

Hate speech, anti-Semitic speech, and Islamophobic speech are all protected by the First Amendment, with several exceptions. Incitement to immediate violence is not protected. Nor is providing material support for designated terrorist groups such as Hamas and Hezbollah. This includes financial contributions that are intended to fall into the hands of a terrorist group.

There is an important legal difference between actions taken by the Department of Education, which is a governmental agency, and those taken by private individuals who bring lawsuits against universities. The government is prohibited from taking any action that compels either a public or a private university to restrict protected free speech. It does not preclude a private citizen from bringing a lawsuit against either a public or a private university for creating or tolerating a hostile environment toward its Jewish students.

A public university can defend its refusal to ban certain speech on its own First Amendment obligations. A private university can claim to be acting in the spirit of the First Amendment, but such a claim might not constitute a complete defense to breach of contract that alleged that a private university ignored its contractual obligation to its students to provide a safe environment.

There are no binding precedents on these complex issues, and the courts will have to make new law balancing conflicting rights—to free speech and to a safe environment.

Universities will not be able to defend against the claim that they are applying a double standard to Jews, as contrasted with other minorities. It is crystal clear that such a double standard exists at most universities. No university would tolerate a Ku Klux Klan club that publicly stated that the lynching of African Americans was justified because they were "uppity." Nor would it permit a sexist club to claim that women who were raped "had it coming" because of how they dressed. Nor would it tolerate public statements that gay or transgender students who were attacked deserved it because of their lifestyles. Yet Harvard and other universities refused to condemn student groups that published letters blaming the Hamas atrocities of October 7 "entirely" on Israel.

The First Amendment requires the government to remain absolutely neutral when it comes to the content of ideas. As Chief Justice William Rehnquist put it in 1990: "Under the First Amendment there is no such thing as a false idea." This means no university that is public or accepts federal funding can seek to distinguish between Jews and other minorities, on the grounds that Jews are somehow "privileged." They must apply precisely the same standard to anti-Jewish or anti-Israel hate speech as they would to anti-Black, anti-feminist, or anti-gay hate speech. It is doubtful that any university today meets that test.

So if a lawsuit can establish that a given university created or tolerates a hostile environment against Jewish students that it would not tolerate against other minority students, that lawsuit might well prevail, even against a First Amendment defense.

W. Jewish Charity Should Prioritize Israel, Jews

Among the most generous contributors to universities, cultural institutions, and general charities have been individual Jews and Jewish family foundations. Jewish philanthropists have made enormous contributions to universities such as Harvard, Penn, Yale, and Columbia. They have contributed to opera houses, museums, symphonies, and ballet. They are major donors to medical centers that treat the general public. They have made significant contributions to Black Lives Matter and other organizations that support minorities, including gay and transgender people. Historically, they have been among the strongest supporters of labor unions.

Of course, many Jews also support Jewish organizations including the United Jewish Appeal and the Jewish National Fund, along with their synagogues and day schools.

Now, Israel, the nation-state of the Jewish people, is in desperate need of charitable and other support. The time has come for Jewish donors to rethink and perhaps reprioritize their charitable giving.

Certain changes in priority seem obvious. No self-respecting Jew should give a penny to any organization that has turned against Israel and supported Hamas. These include Black Lives Matter, the National Lawyers Guild, Jewish Voice for Peace, the Socialist Party, Human Rights Watch, the American Civil Liberties Union, and labor unions that have turned against Israel. These groups should permanently be denied any Jewish charity.

Of course, George Soros will be prioritizing precisely those bigoted groups because he hates Israel and the Jewish people. But he is no model for Jewish giving.

Then there are the American universities such as Harvard, University of Pennsylvania, and Columbia that have done too little, too late to condemn Israel's enemies among their own student body, faculty, and administrators. Jewish donors should stop contributing to these universities unless and until they stop treating Jews worse than they treat other minorities. Few, if any, universities satisfy that test today. Indeed, as a result of the killing of one man—George Floyd—in 2020, many of these institutions have engaged in a massive "reckoning" concerning their treatment of African Americans. Now, as a result of the mass murder of October 7 and the horrible and bigoted reactions to it from within the universities, they must engage in an equally soul-searching and self-critical reckoning about their treatment of Jews and the Jewish state. I am not a wealthy man, but I will not contribute a single penny to City University, Yale, or Harvard—where I went to school—until such a reckoning occurs. I hope others will follow suit.

Finally, there are the cultural, artistic, medical, and other institutions, most of which have taken no position on the recent events in Israel and Gaza. If this is consistent with longstanding policies of not commenting on such events, that is understandable. But if these same institutions have taken actions to support other communities, but not Jews, they, too, are complicit by their selective inaction.

Even regarding those institutions that are not complicit, perhaps the time has come for Jewish donors to prioritize Jewish charitable giving, especially to groups that support Israel and fight anti-Semitism. As famously written in Ecclesiastes, "To everything there is a season." When anti-Semitism and anti-Israel attitudes were on the decline, it was the season for supporting neutral cultural and other institutions. Now, it may be the season for turning a bit more inward.

Rabbi Hillel the Elder taught, "If I am not for myself, who will be for me, but if I am for myself alone, what am I? And if not now, when?" For generations, Jewish philanthropists have emphasized the second part of that sage advice. They should continue to support general institutions, especially medical and social ones that are essential to good health, but for now—when the Jewish community and the Jewish state are in crisis—they should also focus on the first of Hillel's admonitions: we must not neglect ourselves and our own charitable institutions. I, for one, have prioritized my giving to

United Hatzalah, a volunteer emergency medical service that treats Jewish, Muslim, and Christian Israelis alike.

If we ourselves are not for Israel and the Jewish people, who will be?

X. Hamas Massacre Endangers Unity of Democratic Party

The Hamas massacre of October 7, and the international reaction to Israel's military response to it—have been game changers.

They have changed Israel's relationship to Hamas: instead of dealing with it cautiously, the IDF must now totally destroy it. It has changed Israel's relationship to the Gulf States, by threatening the Abraham Accords and the near-term possibility of including Saudi Arabia. It strengthens Israel's relationship with both the Democratic and Republican parties, while at the same time weakening its relationship with progressive and woke Democrats, especially among the young.

It is this third change that threatens the cohesiveness of the Democratic Party as it faces the prospects of close elections in 2024.

The strength of the Democratic Party has always been its ability to represent a wide range of left-leaning voters, ranging from blue-collar workers, to suburban women, to minorities of every sort, to woke progressives, and to Jews. The events of October 7 and the reactions to it, have forever fractured any alliance between centrist liberal Jews and woke progressives.

Since the days of Franklin Delano Roosevelt, Jewish voters could be counted on by the Democratic Party not only to cast their ballots for its candidates, but also to contribute disproportionately to their campaigns. Until recently, the Democratic Party could take for granted the "Jewish vote," with upward of 75 percent of Jews voting for their grandfather's party.

Following the events of October 7, the vast majority of young woke progressives have turned stridently against Israel. Many did so even before Israel responded to the barbarian attacks Hamas levelled against Israeli civilians. It was a knee-jerk, anti-Israel reaction stimulated not by what Israel did—because it had done nothing except be victimized by the Hamas brutality—but what Israel is:

the nation state of the Jewish people. Hard-left Democratic members of Congress voted no or present for a resolution in support of Israel that was overwhelmingly passed. Progressive students at many American universities issued statements, held banners, and participated in marches, not in favor of a two-state solution which would establish a Palestinian state, but rather against the existence of Israel. They were not pro-Palestine; they were anti-Israel. The dominant slogan for these events was "Palestine will be free from the river to the sea." This wish is not ambiguous, for what it means is the ethnic cleansing of all Jewish Israelis from the land of Israel, including the parts of Israel that have been part of the nation state of the Jewish people since its founding. It means a judenrein (free of Jews) Palestine—not a two-state solution, but a final solution for the Jews of Israel.

The breach between Jewish voters who support Israel, even those critical of some of its policies, and the progressives that would end its existence is unhealable. It is also permanent. Never again will Jews who support Israel be willing or able to work together with woke progressives who oppose its very existence.

The Democratic Party will have to make a difficult choice. It's either them or us. There can be no compromise on this issue. As long as Joe Biden is president, the Democrats will continue to side with Israel. But as Tom Freidman of the *New York Times* recently observed: Biden may be the last pro-Israel candidate nominated by the Democratic Party. If future Democratic candidates follow the lead of The Squad, the Democratic Party may well become judenrein. Some Jews will continue to vote for some Democratic candidates, but their allegiance to the party will be weakened to the point of disappearing.

Unlike woke progressives, most centrist Jews have an alternative: they can become moderate centrist Republicans. But that, too, will not be easy, since the Republican Party is quickly moving to the right on issues deeply concerning to many Jews—issues such as abortion rights, gay rights, climate change, gun control, and the Supreme Court. The days of Eisenhower and Rockefeller Republicans—even of Bush Republicans—seems a thing of the past. These movements to extremes within both of these parties leave many Jews feeling politically homeless. That feeling is exacerbated by the reality that we are a two-party nation and there does not seem to be room for the development of a centrist third party representing moderate Democrats who are alienated by the hard left and moderate Republicans who are alienated by the hard right.

Jews, of course, represent only 2.5 percent of Americans, though perhaps a slightly larger percentage of voters, political activists, and contributors. Their drift away from the Democrats may not have an immediate discernable impact on elections, but historically the Jews have been a canary in the mineshaft. And if centrist Jews begin to migrate from the Democratic Party, they are likely to be followed by other moderates. We are already seeing that trend among some Hispanic and Black voters, as well as among working class Blue Dog Democrats.

The events following October 7, was not the only cause of what may eventually be a seismic shift in party affiliations, but they may have exacerbated movements that already were inchoate. These events uncovered some ugly truths that had been suppressed, especially during the political heyday of Donald Trump, whose candidacies since 2016 has solidified Democratic opposition to him. This unity may continue to exist through the 2024 election, but it is likely to disintegrate, especially if Trump is defeated in 2024.

It is possible, of course, that the disruptions caused by the events following October 7, may only be temporary and of passing interest. History moves quickly, especially in the world of the internet. My prediction, however, is to the contrary. I believe the Democratic Party will never be the same following the massive increase in anti-Semitism and anti-Israeli attitudes uncovered by these game-changing events. As Yogi Berra once put it, "It's difficult to make predictions, especially about the future." But predictions about the future are necessary, and my predictions for the Democratic Party—a party I have supported since I first voted for John F. Kennedy in 1960—are dire.

Y. Obama's False Moral Equivalency between Hamas and Israel

Former president Barak Obama has suggested a moral equivalence between the Hamas atrocities of October 7 and Israel's occupation. These are his words:

> That what Hamas did was horrific and there's no justification for it. And what is also true is that the occupation and what's happening to Palestinians is unbearable.

This obscene comparison reflects both ignorance and bias. There can be no possible justification for the beheadings, rapes, burnings, kidnappings, and mass murders of more than fourteen hundred Israeli babies, women, the elderly, and others. Obama has admitted as such. Nor can there be any dispute that these abominations occurred and that Hamas leaders have promised to repeat them again and again.

There are, on the other hand, legitimate justifications—legal, moral, political, and historical—for Israel's continuing military occupation of part of the West Bank, from where terrorists have repeatedly attacked Israeli citizens. The occupation of the Gaza Strip ended in 2005, and control over its borders began only after Hamas began using its population centers as launching pads for rockets and its terror tunnels as underground routes to murder and kidnap Israelis.

Even more important, Israel offered to end the occupation of the West Bank in 2000–2001 and 2008, but the Palestinian leadership did not accept these offers. So, the continuing occupation is at least partially the fault of the Palestinian leadership. The Hamas barbarities were not the fault of Israel, except in the warped minds of the bigoted Harvard students and other anti-Semites who blamed the Hamas rapes and beheadings "entirely" on Israel.

Obama's discussion of the Hamas murders and the Israeli occupation in the same breath lends support to the Harvard and other bigots. It would be as if a southern racist condemned the lynching of Blacks as "horrific" and then immediately criticized African Americans for their high crime rates as also "unbearable." There is simply no comparison between the two and they do not belong in the same paragraph or even on the same page.

The legitimacy of the occupation is very much a matter of degree. Ramallah is not occupied. There are no Israeli troops or civilians in that beautiful thriving and self-governing city. I know. I've been there. Arab residents have more freedom in Ramallah than in most Arab and Muslim cities in Arab countries. Their life there and in other West Bank cities is anything but "unbearable"—and Obama knows it because he, too, has been there.

Gaza City was not occupied after 2005. Its terrible living conditions, even before the current war, were entirely the fault of the Hamas kleptocracy that governs every aspect of life and whose leaders divert funds designed for humanitarian purposes to building rockets and tunnels, and pocketing billions of dollars in their Qatar bank accounts.

The expanding West Bank settlements are controversial, even among most Israelis. But they were not the reason for the Hamas mass murders. It is the very existence of Israel, all of which Hamas claims in its charter is "occupied." Hamas would continue its murderous rampages as long as a single Jew remains "between the river and the sea"—that is, in Tel Aviv, Rishon L'tzion, or Sderot.

Reasonable people can and do disagree about the nature, extent, and justification for Israel's occupation policy and about who has primary responsibility for what Obama describes as "unbearable." No reasonable person can compare it to the murders and rapes committed by Hamas. Yet it is precisely what Obama did. And in doing so, he provided ammunition to Hamas supporters who seek to justify the murders and rapes by pointing to the allegedly "unbearable" conditions under which they live. If a condition is "unbearable," then it follows—at least for some—that there are no limits to what can be done to make it "bearable." That is the claim of Hamas and its supporters, and Obama's ill-advised and deeply immoral comparison lends support to that murderous claim.

Obama's definition of what constitutes illegally occupied territory discloses his long-term bias against the nation state of the Jewish people. As he was leaving office, he supported a United

Nation resolution declaring the Western Wall—the holiest place in Judaism—along with the access roads to Hebrew University and Hadassah Hospital to be illegally occupied. He also regards the unification of Jerusalem to be unlawful and occupied. Fortunately, his extremist views do not reflect America's current policies.

But Obama remains influential within the Democratic Party and especially among young voters. He should immediately retract his dangerous comparison and apologize for his insensitivity toward the victims of the Hamas slaughters.

Z. The World Is Rewarding Hamas's Barbarism and Incentivizing More

The worldwide demonstrations for an Israeli ceasefire are little more than excuses for demanding the end of Israel. The signs and chants disclose the real goals of the organizers and most of the demonstrators. "From the river to the sea, Palestine must be free," does not mean two states. It means one Muslim caliphate with no Jews. So do most of the other demands.

These anti-Israel demonstrations do not include demands to Hamas to free the Israeli hostages, or to stop using Palestinian civilians as human shields. They are not humanitarian, designed to protect all civilian lives. Instead, they are one-sidedly directed only against Israel, and are designed to strengthen Hamas and weaken Israel.

The calls for Israel's demise would persist even if Israel were to agree to a halt in hostilities. The demonstrations might be somewhat smaller, but they would be no less bigoted.

Most American politicians who have expressed anti-Israel sentiments, such as Barak Obama, Bernie Sanders, the Squad, and several Democratic senators, don't call for the end of Israel, but their demands for an unconditional cease fire, with no return of hostages, would lead to the continued ability of Hamas to attack Israel and to reprise their barbaric terrorism against Israeli civilians. Hamas leaders have boasted that October 7 was only the beginning.

The best proof of the real goals of many anti-Israel protesters is that the anti-Israel and pro-Hamas rhetoric began before Israel even attacked Gaza. The recent calls for Palestine to replace Israel were stimulated by the barbarism of October 7, which was seen as a manifestation of Israeli weakness by its enemies, including the Hamas supporters who organized the anti-Israel demonstrations.

These calls, coupled with condemnations of Israel by so many of the international community, sends dangerous messages to Hamas and its supporters: you are winning in the court of public opinion; your plan—to murder Israelis, provoke a reaction by Israel; to place your terrorist assets among civilians who will then die; and to use these deaths to demonize Israel and demand an Israeli surrender—is working, as it has repeatedly in the past. If you do it again, it will work in the future. So why not plan more massacres like October 7? They are a win-win strategy for Hamas.

Israel must not give in to the ill-intentioned pressure of those who are calling for an unconditional ceasefire that would allow Hamas to rearm and regroup. If it does, more Israeli and Palestinian civilians will be killed by the entirely predictable repetitions of Hamas's cynical "dead baby" strategy.

One would expect that rational people would see through this recurring strategy and apply Einstein's purported definition of insanity: "Doing the same thing over and over again and expecting different results." Whether or not Einstein actually spoke these words, they aptly describe the world's repeated reactions to the Hamas strategy: Reward Hamas for its attacks on Israeli civilians; and punish Israel for defending its civilians.

Put more colloquially: wash, rinse, repeat; "Michael Finegan, begin again, begin again"—*ad infinitum*, with increasing deaths.

It may seem counterintuitive and insensitive, but the reality is that allowing Israel to persist in its just goal of eliminating Hamas, even if that requires extensive collateral damage to the human shields currently being exploited by Hamas, will almost certainly result in far fewer civilian deaths in the medium and longer term. The destruction of Hamas will save not only Israeli lives, but also Palestinian lives. It will also improve the quality of life in the Gaza Strip.

Recall that the best thing that ever happened to the German and Japanese people was the total defeat and unconditional surrender of their armies, which came about only after hundreds of thousands of their civilians were killed by allied satiation bombings of densely populated cities. Following these deaths and surrenders, the German and Japanese people became America's best friends. The Middle East is, of course, different than Germany or Japan, but one lesson from the latter may be relevant to the former: immediate deaths of civilians, when tragically necessary to assure defeat of an evil enemy who started the war, may end up doing far more good.

This doesn't mean that noble ends always justify any means. What it does mean is that assuring total victory over an evil regime that kills both its own and enemy civilians with impunity sometimes requires risking the lives of enemy civilians.

Israel should do everything reasonable to minimize civilian deaths, but it should not unreasonably risk its legitimate, and indeed honorable, goals by valuing the lives of enemy civilians—many of whom are complicit in Hamas's crimes—over the lives of its own civilians. So, Israel should categorically reject demands for an unconditional ceasefire designed to strengthen Hamas at the expense of Israel.

AA. Anti-Israel Protests Are Not about Ceasefire

The protests against Israel around the world purport to be demanding a ceasefire, but that is not their real agenda. The not-so-hidden agenda is a demand for the end of Israel and support for Hamas. The protests began the day after the Hamas massacres of fourteen hundred Israelis and the kidnapping of more than two hundred. The early protests supported the massacres and called for the Mideast to be "free" and "clean" of the dirty Jews who live in Israel proper. Those protests against Israel began before the Israeli army responded to the Hamas atrocities, and so they were not motivated by any concern for Palestinian civilians. They supported the murder of Israeli civilians.

Now that Israel is responding, there are new signs and chants demanding a ceasefire that would benefit Hamas. But every single demonstration I have seen also features signs calling for the end of Israel as a genocidal, apartheid, colonialist state. Demonstrators also tear down posters with the pictures and names of Israeli children who were kidnapped by Hamas and are being held as hostages. That too is not about helping Palestinian civilians.

So don't be fooled by so-called "pro-Palestine" or pro-ceasefire protests. The few people who actually join these protests out of such beneficent motives are being used to support the real goals of the organizers: namely the destruction of Israel, the strengthening of Hamas, and the recurrence of the barbarism of October 7.

The reality is that an imposed ceasefire will not save civilian lives. To the contrary, it will cost many more lives in the long run by incentivizing Hamas to repeat the cycle it has perpetuated for decades: kill Israeli civilians; hide Hamas rockets, commanders, and tunnels among Palestinian civilians, hoping that Israel, despite its effort to minimize civilian casualties, will kill some children who are being used as human shields; parade the children in front of television cameras, thereby causing outrage against Israel; force Israel into a ceasefire; and then repeat the process after Hamas rearms and reorganizes.

Leaders of Hamas have already bragged that the slaughters of October 7 were only the beginning. That they will be repeated as long as they benefit from it, as they will if a ceasefire is imposed.

Good people who care about stopping this apparently endless cycle of civilian deaths caused by Hamas should be protesting against the ceasefire and in favor of the total destruction of Hamas. Such a result would be "pro-Palestinian," because Hamas has caused more damage and harm to the Palestinian people than Israel. So anyone who is truly pro-peace, pro-Palestinian, and pro-civilian should be encouraging Israel to finish what Hamas started, by eliminating that terrorist organization from the Gaza Strip.

It may seem counterintuitive to oppose a ceasefire in the interest of reducing civilian casualties, and that is part of the Hamas strategy. It understands that people are more influenced by pictures of dead babies than by logic and experience. They also understand that most people do not think in the long term. Instead, they look for short-term Band-Aids such as ceasefires. But applying a Band-Aid instead of a disinfectant may result in infections.

So the next time you see a demonstration in the local streets, on the university campus, or on television, read the signs carefully. Even if you support a ceasefire or even if you misguidedly support a ceasefire, don't join the demonstration unless you also support Hamas, the end of Israel, and the slaughter and kidnapping of Israeli civilians. Don't be fooled by the anodyne covers that hide the malicious goals of the protests. Don't allow yourself and your good name to be misused by bad people with evil intentions.

These worldwide protests—ill-intentioned as they are—are having an impact on the policy of many nations, most especially the United States. Israelis, who are generally super critical of their government, are not falling for the deceptive nature of these efforts. They know that Hamas seeks to destroy Israel and to do to the millions of Israeli Jews what they already did to fourteen hundred of them. But much of the rest of the world naively assumes that joining a call for a ceasefire is being a do-gooder. It is not. Anyone who joins these protests, whatever their personal views, becomes a do-badder encouraging anti-Semitism and barbarity.

Conclusion to Chapter 1

On October 7, 2023, more Jews were murdered in any one day since the Holocaust. It was worse than a war crime. It was a pogrom, reminiscent of anti-Jewish massacres though history that culminated in the Holocaust. The numbers were not comparable only because Hamas lacked the ability to annihilate Israel's 6.8 million Jews. If they could, they would. If Iran could, it would. If ISIS could, it would. And it would receive the support and acclaim of millions of students and other anti-Jewish bigots throughout the world, who would blame Israel and the Jews.

Following the Holocaust, the world declared "Never again." But it has happened again and again and again—to Africans, Cambodians, and others.

Could it happen again to the Jews and the citizens of their nation state of Israel? I did not think so until the October 7 massacres. Even then, I did not think so. But the reactions at Harvard and other elite institutions that educate our future leaders have caused me to change my mind. I now believe there are many educated Americans and others who would tolerate and even encourage the mass murder of Jewish Israelis in the way that educated Germans—readers of Goethe, listeners of Bach, and students of Heidegger—accepted and facilitated the mass murder of European Jews. When I read about the multiple groups of students that blamed the victims for their murders, rapes, and kidnappings, I realized that some who have declared academic war on the Jews and their state may have been my own students, just as the students of Jewish professors at German universities became fervent Nazis and supported the murders of their teachers. Current students would find or concoct justifications and rationales for their actions and inactions, just as German intellectuals did. They would sleep well and not have regrets, just as the Germans did. Their actions would be explained and justified by self-hating Jews like Norman Finkelstein, Stanley Cohen, and Peter Beinart, just as the actions of the Germans were explained and justified by Gertrude Stein, Alice Toklas, and Hanna Arendt.

Can it happen again? Not in exactly the same way. But the trends today, especially among the young, do not provide assurance against rampant anti-Semitism, dehumanization of Jews, and the immoral double standard against the nation state of the Jewish people, and increasing violence against Jews. These are the ingredients that led to past pogroms and worse. The dynamics must be changed if we are to assure the future of the Jewish people and their state—if we mean it when we say "Never again."

Some American legislators have called on Israel to engage in a cease-fire or pause in its efforts to destroy Hamas. Part of their argument is that failure to do so will just turn Hamas civilians into terrorists. The implication is that if Israel pauses, Gaza citizens will suddenly have more positive views of Israel.

History has proved that friends and allies come from strength, not weakness. After the United States totally devastated Germany and Japan following a total war and unconditional surrender, the Germans and Japanese people became America's closest friends. That would not have happened had a compromise peace been reached. It was the total defeat of Germany and Japan that persuaded its citizens to support the victor.

This is even more true in the Middle East where only strength is respected. The Abraham Accords resulted from Israel being the dominant military, technological, and economic power in the region. Any show of weakness produces enemies, not friends.

The best proof of this reality is that the rise in anti-Semitism and anti-Israel attitudes throughout the world began immediately after Israel's weaknesses were exposed on October 7. The day after fourteen hundred Israelis were murdered, raped, and beheaded, many in the international community and among student groups turned against Israel and against the Jews. They saw weakness and they smelled blood.

Whenever Israel has shown weakness, it has been attacked. Strength is not only the best deterrent against physical attack, but it is also the best way to make friends and influence enemies. A Psalm of David put it very well when it advised that "God will give the Jewish people strength, and then will they get peace." For Israel and for Jews, peace comes only through strength. The more strength, the more peace; the more weakness, the less peace.

The opposite is also true, Hamas gains support when it wins against Israel, even if winning involves rapes, beheadings, and mass murders. The day after these massacres were revealed—even before Israel responded—Hamas received the support of student groups all over the world. Its prestige on the Arab and Muslim street went up dramatically, and its support within Gaza and the West Bank reached an all-time high. Hamas wins by showing strength, even barbarity. Israel loses by showing weakness, even humanitarianism. The net result is that if Israel shows weakness by acceding to the ill-advised demands for a cease-fire, the end result will be more not fewer civilian deaths over time.

The lesson for Israel is clear: the nation-state of the Jewish people must not accept the demands of the international community. It cannot ignore the demands of the United States, but it must remind our leaders and people that Israel has killed far fewer civilians in its effort to destroy Hamas than the Americans and British did in their combined efforts to destroy ISIS and Al Qaeda—threats that were thousands of miles away from their borders, as contrasted to the immediate and proximate threats from Hamas and Hezbollah.

When one group declares war on another, the group declaring war knows that its civilians will suffer. In the case of Hamas this is part of their long-term strategy: kill Israeli civilians, knowing that Israel will respond and kill some Palestinian human shields, including children; display these dead babies to television cameras in the expectation that it will turn world opinion against Israel; this "dead baby strategy" always succeeds and results in Hamas repeating the process over and over again.

Don't take my word for it; listen to Hamas leaders who have already said that what Hamas did to Israeli civilians on October 7, will be repeated endlessly. The only answer to such threats and actions is strength and the destruction of Hamas.

In the end, if Israel is allowed to destroy Hamas without outside pressure, the result will be fewer civilian deaths over time and greater likelihood of peace in the region. Strength begets peace. Weakness begets war. To paraphrase what an Israeli leader said many years ago, if Hamas were to lay down its arms and end its terrorism, there would be peace. If Israel were to lay down its arms, there would be genocide. Take your pick. I know what Israel should do.

Divisions within Israel

———

I n the months leading up to the unprovoked and barbarous attack on Israel, there were considerable divisions among the Israeli people regarding proposals for "judicial reform" that had been put forward by the Netanyahu government. Although the immediate cause of the divisions was these proposals, the divisions were deeper and reflected strong opposition by a very significant proportion of Israelis against the right-wing Likud government, and especially the handful of extremists that Prime Minister Benjamin Netanyahu had to include in his Cabinet in order to get a majority of the Knesset to form a government. Whatever the cause or causes of these divisions, it is clear that they had an impact on reservists, high tech entrepreneurs, the media, and other institutions.

Whether these developments contributed in any way to the decision by Hamas to attack is unclear, especially in light of the reality that the attacks were planned well before these divisions became manifest. What is clear is that the Hamas attack put the divisive domestic issues on the back burner. Nonetheless, the divisions are real and will remain an important reality going forward. It is important, therefore, to understand these factors even while they remain background to the current war in Gaza.

Several of the essays that form subchapters in this chapter were written before the recent war in Gaza, but they remain relevant to what is occurring now, and what is likely to occur when the current war is concluded. Other essays deal more generally with germane issues of anti-Semitism and the concerns of the Jewish community.[1]

---

1   I have updated some of the essays when necessary to be accurate.

CHAPTER 2

The Broader Background

A. Court Packing Undermines Judicial Independence: Both in the US and Israel, the High Court Is under Threat

The specter of court packing is once again rearing its ugly head. Although President Biden has thus far refused to endorse this insidious attempt to destroy the independence of the Supreme Court, many among the growing number of left-wing influencers in the Democratic Party are seeking to gain control over what is supposed to be an independent judiciary under our system of separation of powers.

A recent article in *Medium*, which publishes articles from more mainstream Democrats such as Barack Obama and Hillary Clinton as well as some Republicans, is pulling no punches. It demands that Democrats call for expanding the court in order to put the Justices "on notice that their belligerent intransigence will finally be met with fierce resistance and calls for radical reform."

Following the Supreme Court's ill-advised and unnecessarily broad decision overruling *Roe v. Wade*, many mainstream Democrats, including some influential academics, have sought to expand the number of Justices to fifteen, and to do it immediately so that Biden can nominate the additional six Justices. The *Medium* article declares that "this Supreme Court is poison to its core, thanks to right-wing money, a forty-year campaign by Republican activists such as

Leonard Leo, the Federalist Society and Republican politicians."
It continues; "This is why Democratic leaders need to take a play
from President [Franklin Delano] Roosevelt and at least threaten to
expand the court," or "else conservative Justices will simply double
down on their ideological crusade."

This left-wing campaign to take over the Supreme Court will
only increase if and when the Justices end race-based affirmative
action, as they are likely to do this term. [They did it in June 2023]
Fortunately for our separation of powers, court packing remains
unlikely to be achieved so long as the Republicans control one house
of Congress.

Let there be no mistake about it: attempts to pack the court and
weaken it in other ways are not designed to bring about structural
improvement in the court's workings. They are designed solely
to achieve immediate political ends, namely ensuring Supreme
Court decisions that favor the left and the Democratic Party. On
their merits, I would support many of these outcomes. As a liberal
Democrat, I yearn for the Supreme Court for which I clerked back
in the 1960s, which expanded civil rights, freedom of speech, separation of church from state, the rights of the accused, and other
basic liberties. But I strongly oppose using structural reforms to
achieve these ends.

The mirror image of this left-wing attempt to weaken our Supreme
Court is being played out in Israel, where the political shoe is on
the other foot. In Israel it is the right-wing that is dissatisfied with
decisions rendered by its Supreme Court, and so it is trying to take
control over the appointment process. This is akin to court packing,
since the goal is the same: to appoint a majority of Justices that support the political and ideological goals of those seeking reform.

The major difference is that the court-packing proposals in the
United States have received little attention. The debate has been
largely academic. In Israel, on the other hand, the proposed reforms
have led to some of the largest and most divisive demonstrations in
Israeli history.

Why the difference? The public outcry against the proposed
reforms in Israel reflect a deeper dissatisfaction with the current

Israeli right-wing government. Many who strongly oppose these proposed reforms also strongly oppose Benjamin Netanyahu and his Likud coalition. It is different in the United States where the Democratic Party controls the White House and the Senate.

The point is that judicial reform, whether in the United States or in Israel, is not the kind of issue that generally incites the public and provokes angry demonstrations. It is largely a symptom of a deeper dissatisfaction with those in charge. Israel is a parliamentary democracy, and such democracies do not have the kind of separation of powers that the United States has. Separation of powers diffuses protests because each major party controls some branches. In the United States, the Republican Party controls the House and the Supreme Court, whereas the Democratic Party controls the Senate and the executive. In Israel, Netanyahu's right-wing coalition controls both the executive and legislative functions, and now seeks to take more control over the judiciary.

Judicial reforms, if it is to occur, should be based on solving long term institutional problems, not on the partisan desire for immediate changes in judicial outcomes. But the tragedy is that in the US and Israel—which are deeply divided politically and ideologically—both sides want to achieve their immediate goals, without much regard for future implications.

B. Fewer Minority and Civil Rights Will Weaken Liberty, Not Democracy

In the ongoing debate over reforms designed to weaken the Supreme Court of Israel, there is considerable confusion about their effect on democracy, as distinguished from minority rights and civil liberties. Democracy, legally defined, means majority rule. Israel will remain a parliamentary democracy in which a fairly elected majority decides fundamental issues of policy, even if ill-advised judicial reforms are enacted.

It will not become like apartheid South Africa or authoritarian Turkey or Hungary, where minority dictators make the decisions. It will, however, become a democracy less sensitive to minority rights and civil liberties.

In an important respect, there is an inherent conflict between democracy and the protection of minority rights. When the rights of minorities prevail over the will of the majority—as they should in certain areas, such as free speech and the non-establishment of religion—democracy is compromised.

The United States, for example, is not a democracy. It is a republic with structural checks on democracy. The Electoral College, the Senate, and the Bill of Rights are all part of our counter-majoritarian system of checks and balances designed to limit the excesses of majority rule when it comes to conflict with minority rights, such as free speech for unpopular dissents.

Nor is Israel a pure democracy with or without the proposed judicial changes. The threshold for Knesset qualification, the reality of the coalition system, the role of the security cabinet and other constraints on simple majority rule make it like other parliamentary systems: essentially but not completely democratic. Indeed, since the time of Athens, there has not been a perfect democracy.

In some such systems, the courts can review and overrule parliamentary votes and in some, they can't. In some, the parliament can override judicial decisions and in others, it can't. Permitting an override or denying judicial review does not make parliamentary democracies undemocratic or tyrannical; it merely makes them less sensitive to minority rights and civil liberties. It is a matter of striking the right balance.

Different democracies strike the balance between majority and minority rights differently. Israel has generally struck it quite appropriately during its first seventy-five years. The proposed judicial reform threatens to skew the balance away from minority rights and civil liberties. It is, of course, largely a matter of the degree to which reasonable citizens can and do differ. But it is an important matter of degree that may shape the future of Israel.

Both in the United States and in Israel, the power of the judiciary to overrule legislative—of the majority—decisions is under attack. The hard left in America is trying to weaken the current Supreme Court by packing it, limiting its jurisdiction, and imposing term and/ or age limits.

The current attack has been stimulated by a series of high court decisions that favor the right. In Israel, the attack is based on decisions that purportedly favor the left.

In both instances, wrongheaded and permanent structural changes are being proposed in response to short-term dissatisfaction with the current directions of the courts. In both instances, the so-called reforms will endanger the checks and balances that help democracies govern fairly. In both instances, they should be opposed by those who favor democracy, minority rights, and civil liberties.

They should also be opposed by those who case about Israel's standing in the international community and especially before the International Criminal Court and other judicial and quasi-judicial bodies. To be sure, Israel will continue to be subjected to a double standard regardless of what it does.

But those of us who defend Israel in these bodies, as well as in the court of public opinion, have long relied on a strong Supreme Court that protects human rights. We will continue to defend Israel against unfair attacks, but our job will become even harder if the judiciary and civil liberties are weakened.

There are reforms that can be enacted without harming civil liberties. The jurisdiction of the Supreme Court could be reduced over essentially political issues, such as the gas deal with Lebanon or whether particular politicians are eligible to serve in the government. If an override were limited to these and other non-civil liberties issues, they would be less objectionable, but if a simple Knesset majority could override the judicial protection of fundamental rights such as equality, due process, free speech and the like, Israel would be the worse for it.

Today such an override may help the right; tomorrow it may hurt the right.

C. Why Is the World Obsessed with Israeli Judicial Reform?

A strident debate is occurring in Israel about the role of the judiciary and democratic governance. Virtually every democracy debates this issue periodically because there is an inherent conflict between majority power and minority rights.

The traditional role of non-elected courts is to impose a check on politicians who are elected by the majority. Whenever courts over-rule decisions reached by the majority, there are complaints. This has been true in the United States since the days of Thomas Jefferson and John Marshall. The United States Supreme Court's decision in the Dred Scott case was one of the causes of the American Civil War, and its decision in Brown vs. Board of Education led to the wide-spread demands for the impeachment of Chief Justice Earl Warren throughout the South. Sometimes, history has proved the courts to be right, as in the Brown case; many times, history has proved the courts to be wrong, as in Dred Scott, the detention of Japanese Americans during World War II, and the compelled sterilization of the mentally ill in the 1920s.

There is no perfect solution to the paradox of appointed judges overruling elected legislators, but some strike a better balance than others.

Israel is now in the midst of one of the most contentious debates in its history. Israel is different from the United States in that in its foundation it was far closer to being a pure democracy than our republic. The Knesset is a single house legislature. The executive is part of the legislature and serves at its will. Israel has no written constitution. Israel's only mechanism for checks and balances is the judiciary, which itself is a creature of the Knesset and thus subject to Knesset control and limitations.

Throughout Israel's seventy-five-year history, and especially since the 1990s, the Supreme Court has served as an effective check on the excesses of the Knesset, the prime minister, the military, and other institutions of government. Some think that its checks have been excessive. This is especially the attitude among those who support emerging right-wing populism, reflected most dramatically in the most recent election and the current government, which includes some religious and nationalist extremists. They oppose what has been called the "judicial revolution" of the 1990s and are seeking a counter-revolution of their own that would significantly curtail the powers of the Supreme Court. The majority of Israelis seem to be somewhere in the middle, opposing both the extreme reforms of the new government and what many regard as the excesses of the earlier judicial revolution.

As an outsider who has been deeply involved in defending Israel for more than half a century, I am concerned about this clash of extremes and have been seeking to propose compromise resolutions that are acceptable, if not desired, by both sides. I've spoken to leaders of both camps as well as those in the middle. These include Prime Minister Benjamin Netanyahu, former Supreme Court president Aharon Barak, President Isaac Herzog, Knesset members Itamar Ben-Gvir and Bezalel Smotrich, as well as many academics. The law professor in me loves this debate. But the divisions that it seems to be causing, or at least reflecting, is worrying. I hope I can contribute even a very small amount to helping resolve or narrow the differences, since I have close friends on both sides, and the rights and wrongs are not limited to one side.

What intrigues me most is why the world is paying so much attention to what is essentially a domestic Israeli dispute. The world paid little attention when left-wing Democrats demanded the packing of the US Supreme Court and limitations on the terms and powers of the Justices following the controversial overturning of *Roe v. Wade*. Even when President Joe Biden appointed a commission to study these issues and make recommendations, the international community ignored it.

But the world seems obsessed with the Israeli debate, as it does about so many other issues relating to Israel. This obsession is part of the dangerous double standard that the international community has long imposed on the nation state of the Jewish people. The centrality of Israel to the major religions may explain the focus of the adherents to these faiths, but it does not explain the obsession of the secular left. Nearly everything Israel does generates criticism from international bodies and organizations. These groups devote more attention to Israel than to the rest of the nations of the world combined. And this international attention is often used and misused by Israeli advocates against their opponents. For example, in the current debate, opponents of the judicial reforms have argued that if they are enacted it will cause international businesses to leave Israel. This may well become a self-fulfilling prophecy, as economics is often a question of perception rather than reality.

Both sides have tried to weaponize members of the American Jewish community to pressure the other side. I am an opponent of most of the proposed reforms, though I think that a compromise on some of them is in order. But let's be clear: even if all the proposed reforms are enacted (which I hope they will not be) Israel will remain a strong democracy. It will remain far more democratic than any other countries in the region and also more democratic than most European and Asian countries. Indeed, the reforms would bring Israel closer to being a pure democracy governed by majority rule. But they would endanger minority rights, civil liberties, equal rights, due process, and the rule of law. That's why I oppose them. Israel would be a better democracy with these principles kept intact than if they are compromised by a reduction in the power of the Supreme Court to enforce them.

The international community has little or no stake in the outcome of this debate. It will have little effect, if any, on any peace process or on the Abraham Accords or on Israel's relationships with other countries. The recent election itself, and the new government it produced, may well impact relations with the Palestinians and others, and the ill-advised judicial reforms seem to be serving as a surrogate for these more international concerns. Even the mass demonstrations against the judicial reforms in Tel Aviv and Jerusalem often go beyond that issue and extend to general opposition to the new government and its right-wing policies. These demonstrations are the best evidence of Israel's commitment to the democratic values of peaceful protest against a democratically elected government that is wildly unpopular among large and influential members of the public. Democracy produced the new government, and democracy produced the protests against it. So much for the fearmongering among those who are telling the world that Israel is on the verge of becoming an autocracy—or in the false and dangerous words of some extremists, that it has already become the Germany of the 1930s.

Even back in 2016, that false comparison was being made.[2]

Israel may continue to move rightward, as many other countries have in the growing age of nationalism and populism. For the first several decades of its existence it veered to the left, with elements of socialism. Changing demography changes politics. That's democracy. But I don't believe that the Israeli people will easily succumb to the temptations of authoritarianism—and certainly not fascism. They are too independent, opinionated, and ornery. They have chutzpah, in the best sense of that term. More importantly, and more relevant to this discussion, if the pendulum were ever to swing in the direction of fascism—which I do not believe it will—the Supreme Court alone will not save it.

As the great American jurist Learned Hand observed in his "Spirit of Liberty" speech of 1944, during a war of fascism against democracy, "I often wonder whether we do not rest our hopes too much upon constitutions, upon laws and upon courts. These are false hopes; believe me, these are false hopes. Liberty lies in the hearts of men and women; when it dies there, no constitution, no law, no court can even do much to help it. While it lies there it needs no constitution, no law, no court to save it."

I think Judge Hand may have understated the possible influences of the judiciary on helping to preserve liberty, but he was certainly correct to place more emphasis on the "hearts and minds of men and women." The current protests against weakening the judiciary speak loudly about the spirit of liberty among so many Israelis.

Israel should do the right thing not because of pressure from other nations, but because it is best for Israel. The international obsession with Israel's imperfections does not promote the spirit of Liberty among Israelis. The conflict over judicial reform must be solved by Israelis based on Israeli values. Outsiders must feel free to offer advice but should refrain from trying to put undue pressure on Israeli democratic decision-making. I am confident that Israel's values will be its "Iron Dome" against authoritarianism.

2　See "Israel General Compares Modern Israel to 1930s Germany," *Middle Eastern Eye*, May 5, 2016.

D. The Israel Protests Are About Netanyahu, Not Democracy

The judicial reforms may be a bad idea, but their consequences would not be so catastrophic.

Why has the diaspora been shouting so loudly about the Israeli government's judicial reforms recently? Answer: Netanyahu.

The thousands of people in America and Europe who are rallying against legislative change in the Jewish state, changes with which I mostly disagree, do not really care about the proposals themselves, much less understand them. What they care about are the people behind them.

If the same proposals had been put forward by moderate centrists, they would not have generated this type of opposition. When I've spoken to Americans who've been involved in the demonstrations, they are certainly unable to explain in any convincing detail why they are out on the streets.

And I'm not surprised. In my sixty years as a lawyer and professor, I have never seen a single protest against judicial reform in the US. The same goes for Europe: What do the people of that continent care about judicial reform in Israel? These are protests against an Israeli prime minister and government they do not like.

Moreover, even if all the things that are being proposed were enacted, Israel's judicial system would simply resemble that of Britain, Canada, and, to some extent, America.

In fact, most countries in the world have judges appointed by the government and many countries grant their soldiers some kind of immunity. Moreover, very few have the kind of judicial review that Israel currently has.

So, what we're actually talking about, potentially, is Israel becoming like many countries, or as it was a half-century ago. Do I want this? I do not. I think Israel should be better than other countries, a better democracy.

But if these proposed laws are enacted, if the power of the Israeli courts is curbed somewhat, its judicial system will simply resemble those of New Zealand, Australia, France, Italy, and other democratic states.

Sure, the changes would compromise Israel's commitment to minority rights, to civil liberties and free speech, and these are not things I wish to see.

But they would not compromise the country's democracy. In virtually every parliamentary democracy in the world, parliament rules. It has the last word.

The truth is, Israelis, primarily on the left, have come to expect too much from their courts as a result of the activism of the past thirty years.

Meanwhile, their country's credibility is being badly damaged by the protests. Extremists on both sides in Israel seem to just want to win the argument, and the truth is, right now, the extremes of sides are winning.

And if you're winning, why give up?

These protests, from both sides, while entirely lawful and part of democracy, have the potential to do enormous damage to what Israelis have worked so hard for since the foundation of the state in 1948.

There is a solution, of course. Israelis should listen to President Isaac Herzog, whose talks with both sides have been slowly moving ahead, pushing for a compromise agreement.

Herzog is operating above the political fray, positioning himself as a mediator rather than a decision-maker in his attempts to bring about agreement between Netanyahu's coalition and his opposition.

The president is not proposing specifics, he is trying to bring people to the bargaining table.

But will the extremists on either side listen? I doubt it. The right won't come to the bargaining table because they think too much compromise will damage their standing. The left won't listen because the protests have strengthened their political base.

And who is losing out? The people of Israel, the vast majority of whom the president speaks for.

E. With All This Infighting, the Real Loser Is Israel

The time has come to come to the bargaining table and hammer out a deal.

Among my two oldest friends in Israel are former president of the Supreme Court Aharon Barak and current prime minister Benjamin Netanyahu.

It is not surprising, therefore, that I see some virtue on both sides of the debate. But I also believe that both sides have exaggerated the faults of the other.

The two major issues are the proposals that the Knesset, by a simple majority, should be able to overrule nearly all Supreme Court decisions; and judges should be selected by a modified committee controlled by politicians.

It would be a serious mistake to allow the Knesset to override all Supreme Court decisions, including those that protect minority rights, due process, freedom of speech and other core liberties. But that doesn't mean the court should have the last word on who can serve in the government and other political and economic matters.

Some form of Knesset override might well be appropriate in such cases. It may also be appropriate to eliminate the current veto that judges have over Supreme Court appointments, while assuring that the majority are professionals, not politicians.

Both sides have exaggerated the consequences of not getting their way. Some on the right argue that unless the Knesset can override the Supreme Court, democracy will be subordinated by an elite, unelected institution.

History shows otherwise. In several democracies, including the US, the Supreme Court gets the last word on core issues of liberty, subject only to constitutional amendments, which are very difficult to enact. These countries still preserve their core democratic character, while also protecting minorities, due process, and free speech.

Some on the right also argue that unless Justices are nominated through a political process, the court will remain elitist and undemocratic.

But many countries have mixed systems of appointing judges that include large elements of professionalism and elitism. Indeed, it is the proper function of a supreme court to serve as a check on current popular opinion.

On the other side of the argument, some insist that the proposed changes would end Israel as a democracy and turn it into an authoritarian state. They too are wrong.

Although I disagree with most of the proposals, I do not believe that they would end Israel's long-standing status as a vibrant democracy. They would, however, endanger some basic liberties and unpopular rights.

I strongly support President Herzog's call to compromise. Each side must give up some of their demands and accept some from the other side. The key is to preserve the independence of the Supreme Court as a nonpartisan and nonpolitical institution.

In my private discussions with both sides, there is willingness to compromise. But in public, they tend to maintain their positions because the extremists on both sides of this contentious debate are winning.

Opponents of the reforms have generated enormous grassroots support, while extremists on the right are solidifying their bases and benefitting from the divisions.

The real losers are the majority of centrist Israelis who support some reform but not all of the proposals, and the State of Israel itself, which is suffering grievously on the international stage and in the diaspora. The time will soon be ripe to come to the bargaining table and hammer out a compromise

F. Bibi Left Out the Most Important Part

It was an honor to be quoted by Prime Minister Benjamin Netanyahu during his statement about the proposed judicial reforms. He quoted my words accurately, but he omitted the thrust of my central message: That further compromise is absolutely necessary.

I remain opposed to both the original and revised proposals because they cross two red lines: 1) they permit the Knesset by a simple majority to override Supreme Court decisions guaranteeing fundamental minority rights, freedom of speech, and due process; and 2) they empower a majority of politicians, rather than professionals, to select future Justices.

The prime minister correctly quoted me as denying that, if enacted, these wrongheaded reforms would turn Israel into an anti-democratic authoritarian state. Israel will remain democratic as long as a majority of its citizens can elect its leaders in a fair vote. Israeli voters would never tolerate an autocracy. They are for too argumentative and opinionated to take orders from a dictator.

Although Israel will remain a vibrant democracy, it would be a far better democracy if the Supreme Court had the power to check and balance the majority regarding open unpopular basic rights. Recall that many of the most basic rights—such as freedom of speech and due process for hated people—are unpopular with a majority of voters, but essential to the rule of law.

It is important to remember that many western democracies do not have checks and balances based on the separation of powers. Nor do they authorize judicial review of legislative decisions. Parliamentary supremacy is the rule rather than the exception.

But Israel has had a better democracy than most, precisely because the Supreme Court has enforced basic minority rights even when a temporary majority has sought to violate them. So, it is important to try to maintain the benefits of the current Israeli system, while not exaggerating the likely implications of a negative change. Unfortunately, each side has overstated the dangers of the other side's positions being accepted.

G. Israel's Supreme Court: One of the Best in the World

The Supreme Court of Israel has long been the envy of most other democratic nations precisely because it vigorously enforces the rule of law even against the sometimes popular will. It is regarded as one of the best supreme courts in the world and its Justices as among the most highly regarded. That is why it has served as Israel's legal "Iron Dome" against biased attempts by international courts to selectively target its soldiers and military commanders. These "reforms," even with proposed softening changes, would reduce this protection.

On the other hand, there are some reforms that are consistent with my red lines and the preservation of basic rights and judicial independence. These include permitting Knesset overrides of decisions that are primarily political, such as who can serve in the government, or economic, such as the reasonableness of the Lebanon gas deal.

Similarly, eliminating the current veto judges have over their successors would be acceptable, as long as the selection remains in the hands of professionals rather than politicians. Prime Minister Netanyahu cites the American mechanism for selecting justices—presidential nomination, Senate confirmation—as support for his proposal. But the American process has politicized and degraded our Supreme Court. It is anything but a model that Israel should emulate.

These are not the only compromises that might go a long way toward satisfying—or at least being tolerable to—both sides. Many other reasonable compromises have been proposed by centrist left- and right-leaning Zionists. But unfortunately, compromise is unlikely in the present environment because the extremes of both sides are winning.

The left is energizing voters with its mass demonstrations, while the right is strengthening its base. The losers are the majority of centrist Israelis who seek an end to this divisive stalemate, as well as the relationship between Israel and the outside world, including Diaspora Jews and the international community.

Unfortunately, the world is obsessed with focusing on Israeli imperfections and divisions. The proposed reforms, whether good or bad, are essentially a domestic matter, but when Israel is involved, nothing stays at home. Both sides are seeking support from outsiders, which magnifies the divisions and makes a compromise resolution more essential.

I hope that if the prime minister were to quote me again, he will repeat my call for both sides to sit down with President Herzog and others without any preconditions, and reach compromises which each side can accept—if not love. That is my essential message.

H. Israeli Democracy's Vibrance Is Again on Display

Israel remains among the most vibrant democracies in the world today.

No democracy has had more transforming elections and more successful demonstrations than Israel. The recent turnabout in the Netanyahu government's plan to rush through a one-sided judicial "reform" is just the latest example of Israel's raucous democracy at work. Those who fear that Israel is on the path to autocracy need only observe recent events in that nation's history.

No country has a freer or more critical press and media than Israel, especially with regard to political controversies. Although there are limits on the publication of some national security secrets, the media has figured out how to evade military censorship by laundering the secrets through foreign reporters. In actual practice, there is no country that publishes information more critical of the government than Israel.

Nor are there many countries whose universities are more one-sidedly antagonistic to the government. Yet they operate freely with government financial support.

Neither is there any country that has a more contentious parliament than the Knesset.

The ultimate check on authoritarianism is, of course, the citizenry, which can bring about changes in government by fair and free elections. Israel has had more such elections than any other nation since 1996. As noted earlier, the great judge Learned Hand observed during World War II: "Liberty lies in the hearts of men and women; when it dies there, no constitution, no law, no court can save it."

The Israeli people are too argumentative, opinionated, and ornery for liberty to die in their hearts. The Jewish people, which comprise the majority of Israelis, have too long a history of being oppressed by tyrants ever to tolerate autocracy. Israel, like England, lacks a written constitution of the kind other countries have. But like England, it has a tradition of civil liberties that serves as an effective protection.

There are, to be sure, certain components of Israeli society that are undemocratic. A small number of very religious Jews believe that Israel should not be a secular democratic state but rather a biblical theocracy. The number of these fundamentalists is growing, but they remain a tiny portion of the population. Because of Israel's coalition system, their voices are somewhat magnified, and they have disproportionate influence over the current government. That, too, is part of democracy: giving voice to undemocratic elements in an otherwise democratic polity. There are also those ultra-nationalists who, while insisting on democracy in Israel, would deny it to Palestinians on the West Bank. That too is part of Israeli internal democracy: giving voice to those who would deny democracy to others. They too have disproportionate influence in West Bank policy, but not necessarily on policies involving Israel itself.

These issues are complex, as is the nature of democracy in a polity that calls itself the nation-state of the Jewish people, and whose Declaration of Independence guarantees equality to its non-Jewish citizens. There can be, and are, divisive debates about the nature of democracy in so complex a context. But at its core democracy means that important policies are determined by a majority vote of the citizens. That has never been challenged with regards to Israel. Arab citizens—both Muslim and Christian—have equal rights to vote. Their political parties, which have joined past Israeli governments, are increasingly influential.

The proposed reforms, which led to the demonstrations and Prime Minister Benjamin Netanyahu's recent pause, would not, even if enacted in full, end democracy in Israel. They might, however, result in a reduction of minority rights and the rights of dissenters to free speech and due process. These negative consequences would be caused by the power of the Knesset to override Supreme Court decisions that have hereto protected those rights. Rejecting these reforms therefore would keep Israel a better democracy, but Israel will remain a vibrant democracy even if all these ill-advised reforms were to be enacted.

I. What Makes Israeli Protests Different from Other Protests?

Israel is embroiled in the largest and most contentious protests in its seventy-five-year history. Nearly every weekend for several months now, tens of thousands of strident opponents of the current government's proposals for so-called judicial reform have gathered in squares in major cities. There have been smaller counterprotests as well from supporters of the reforms.

Speeches by respected personalities have ranged from scholarly to strident, from credible to exaggerated, from constructively critical to outrageously mendacious, from optimistic to angrily pessimistic, from loving of Israel to hatred of the nation-state of the Jewish people.

Equally important to what has been said and done at these demonstrations is what has not been said and done. There has been little or no call for unlawful violence, there have been no deaths or serious injuries, there have been few arrests, and most important there have been no efforts by the government to stop the anti-government protests. There is no guarantee that as anger percolates there will not be some violence, but up to now most of the demonstrations have been conducted peacefully.

Contrast these relatively peaceful protests with demonstrations in other countries. The Arab Spring was rife with violence, including deaths, serious injuries, molestation of women, and many arrests and beatings by government agents. In Iran, protesters were executed and beaten to death. Even in America, Black Lives Matter protests included shootings, massive property destruction, and arrests.

Israeli protests have been models of civility, with few exceptions. Israel is teaching the world how to conduct loud, belligerent, and angry demonstrations against and in favor of controversial government proposals and actions within the rules of law and the constraints of democracy. And these nonviolent protests have not been ineffective. They have resulted in the postponement of some of the protested governmental actions and encouraged ongoing efforts to seek compromises. Government offcials are listening and responding.

The leaders and participants in these massive protests are to be commended for the manner in which they are expressing their deeply felt anger. And government offcials should be commended as well for their nonprovocative responses. These protests demonstrate democracy at work. They also demonstrate that democracy will never be in danger of turning to autocracy in a nation like Israel, that encourages dissent and disagreement.

The spirit of liberty is alive and well throughout Israel. Reasonable Israelis believe that Israeli democracy will be undercut if the proposed reforms are allowed to weaken the Supreme Court. Other reasonable Israelis believe that the extensive power of the unelected Justices compromises liberty and democracy. Most Israelis agree with President Isaac Herzog that extremists on both sides are exaggerating the stakes and that compromises are possible and would be beneficial. I am in that camp. But I also believe that even if all the government proposals were to be adopted, democracy and liberty would continue to thrive among the opinionated and contentious citizens of Israel. I oppose some of the proposed reforms because I believe they endanger minority rights and some civil liberties that are now enforced by the Supreme Court. But the impact of these reforms—ill-advised as some may be—are considerably exaggerated by many of their opponents. They would make Israel more like Great Britain, Canada and even the United States, and not at all like Hungary, Poland, and Turkey.

The current Supreme Court, absent any of the reforms, is the most powerful and influential Supreme Court among current democracies. It is also somewhat self-perpetuating, because the commission that appoints new Justices allocates an effective veto to current Justices. It is the only court, of which I am aware, that has no requirement that petitioners have "standing" to bring the case—that is, that they are uniquely affected by the laws or procedures they challenge. This means that non-government organizations and even external groups can bring lawsuits challenging Israeli laws. It is also the only court I know of that strikes down political and economic rules on the ground that they are extremely unreasonable. American courts used to do something similar during the New Deal under the rubric of substantive due process, which was roundly criticized, especially by liberals. But despite these controversial attributes, the Supreme Court of Israel has done much good for the country and is among the most respected high courts in the world.

These peaceful protests have garnered support throughout Europe and the United States, even among Jewish supporters of Israel, despite the reality that the proposed judicial reform is largely a domestic issue with little impact outside the borders of Israel. Whatever Israel does seems to receive disproportionate attention from the international community. Little attention has been devoted to the praiseworthy nature of Israeli protests and the government's unprovocative reaction to them.

Democracy is too deeply embedded in the hearts of most Israelis for autocracy ever to take root in that young nation.

J. Protests about the Judiciary, American and Israeli Style

The right to protest is central to any democracy. Our First Amendment guarantees the right of the people to peaceably assemble and to petition the government for a redress of grievances. Protests in democracies are generally directed against executive and legislative actions, rarely against the judicial branch.

This is because generally in democracies, the judiciary plays a limited role in the lives of its citizens and so citizens rarely have much to protest about. But in both the United States and Israel, where their Supreme Courts are more activist, protests against judicial decisions have taken center stage.

In the US, the high court's decision overruling *Roe v. Wade* has generated strident protests, some directed personally against the Justices who voted against a woman's right to choose. An armed man was caught near the home of Justice Brett Kavanaugh shortly before the decision was announced but after it had been leaked. His goal may have been to assassinate the Justice whom he believed would cast the swing vote against *Roe v. Wade*. Fortunately, he was arrested before he could do any harm.

Peaceful but deeply annoying protests have frequently been conducted in front of the homes of Justices. Section 1507 of the Criminal Code prohibits such protests if they are intended to influence judicial decisions. Here's what the statute provides: "Whoever, with the intent of interfering with, obstructing or impeding the administration of justice or with the intent of influencing any judge, juror, witness or court offcer, in the discharge of his duty, pickets or parades near [a] residence occupied or used by such judge, juror, witness or court offcer . . . shall be fined . . . or imprisoned not more than one year or both."

Some judges and scholars have raised constitutional concerns about the applicability of this statute to Justices of the Supreme

Court and other appellate judges appointed with a life tenure. They are deemed to be immune from the pressures of protests, whereas trial judges and jurors are far more likely to be influenced by protests.

These constitutional concerns may explain why the Justice Department has been unclear about whether to prosecute peaceful protesters who frequently appear in front of the homes of Justices, in violation of the explicit terms of this statute, but perhaps are engaging in constitutionally protected protests.

For the most part, protests directed against American judges and other public offcials have been peaceful. Occasionally, however, protests have gotten out of hand and have caused violence against people and property, including occasional deaths. Protests in other countries, such as France and the Netherlands, have been more violent.

What are the possible explanations for these differences?

Some might argue that the underlying causes of these protests justify, or at least explain, the more frequent violence in France and the United States compared with Israel.

The former protests were about unjust killings of minority citizens, while the latter are about more abstract issues of justice.

But Israelis also regard their protests as involving life-and-death issues, such as the proper role of courts in constraining military and police responses to terrorism against innocent civilians and the obligation of all citizens to risk their lives by being drafted into military service.

The stakes are high in all these protests in different parts of the world. But the level of violence is quite different.

Another possible explanation may be found in the fact that the protesters themselves are different in the different countries.

In Israel, they cross ethnic, religious, and even political lines.

Although many of the protesters are secular, Ashkenazi (of European heritage), residents of Tel Aviv and anti-Netanyahu, a considerable number are religious, Sephardi (of Middle Eastern heritage), residents of Jerusalem and conservative.

Brothers, sisters, neighbors, and friends are on different sides of the protests and counterprotests.

In France, and to a somewhat lesser degree in the United States, the protesters tended to be members of disaffected minority groups with grievances against the country as a whole and its institutions.

"Their goals are to destabilize our republican institutions and bring blood and fire down on France," the interior minister said of a previous protest this year, while "Burn it all down!" has been a frequent slogan at US demonstrations.

Most of the Israeli protesters, on the other hand, are Zionists who love their country and are trying to prevent policies they believe will damage their beloved Israel.

The last thing they want to do is harm their country, though some of the protesters have advocated mischief that would hurt the high-tech economy and even the military.

Whatever the reasons, there are no justifications for the violence of the French and some American protests.

The three great democracies—the United States, Israel, and France—are increasingly fractured and divided along political, religious, and racial lines.

There will be more protests as the divisions get worse and as often-unpredictable events serve as provocations.

The democratic world should learn from Israel that protests can be an important aspect of democratic governance—as long as they remain nonviolent.

K. Israel Is Being Attacked by Political Short Sellers

The newest weapon in the campaign against the ill-advised and overreaching judicial "reforms" being advocated by some Israeli politicians is the equally ill-advised and overreaching effort by some opponents to endanger Israel's economy.

They claim that the judicial reform proposals, if enacted, would make Israel a less lucrative venue in which to invest. There is, though, nothing in the proposals themselves that would have any direct negative impact on Israel's economy in general or on the "startup nation" aspect of its high-tech sector.

It is the false claim itself—not the true workings of the economy—that is affecting the economic standing of the nation-state of the Jewish people. This is an example of a self-fulfilling prophecy, in which the prediction itself, even if baseless or overstated, can hurt a company or a country.

Short sellers have long been aware of this phenomenon, and some have used (misused?) it to their unfair advantage. They spread false rumors in the hope and expectation that their rumors will lower the prices of stocks they are shorting. That is analogous to what some opponents of judicial reform are trying to do in an effort to create pressure against the proposed reforms.

It may be working, at least in the short run. Some companies have threatened to pull their investments, and Israel's credit rating has been downgraded. These actions are not a direct result of the judicial reforms themselves. They are more a function of the alleged instability reflected in the demonstrations and counterdemonstrations, as well as in the frequency of Israeli elections and the appointment of extremists to the recently organized Netanyahu government. These alleged manifestations of "instability" are the best evidence that Israel is a thriving democracy. France too has demonstrations and extremists, but they are not seen as reasons to doubt that country's democratic character.

Israel is a stable democracy that is undergoing demographic, political, religious, and other changes. It is dealing with these changes democratically, by elections, demonstrations, debates, and (hopefully) compromises. Israel is not Hungary, Poland, Slovakia, or Turkey, where autocracy has long been the norm.

Israel, on the other hand, has a seventy-five-year history of raucous but generally nonviolent disputation. Israel is much more like the United States, which is also deeply divided politically, racially, regionally, and religiously.

The most recent Israeli demonstrations have been models of nonviolence, especially as compared with other democracies. Israel has a free press, academic freedom, and among the most opinionated citizens in the world. The press and academia are ferociously anti-government for the most part, and the government rarely tries to interfere with their right to criticize it.

The compromises currently under consideration seem to recognize the need to preserve the Supreme Court's legitimate power in

these areas. In recent interviews, Prime Minister Netanyahu has suggested that he is open to compromises that produce "balance."

The appropriate balance between democratic majority rule and
minority rights is always a diffcult one to strike, and reasonable people can and do disagree in many democratic countries. This has been
evidenced most recently in the United States by decisions regarding
a woman's right to choose abortion in states where a majority opposes
that right, or decisions involving race-based affirmative action.

There is no good reason for opponents of the reform to deploy
the unfair weapon of endangering the economy of Israel by creating
self-fulfilling prophecies that hurt all Israelis and weaken its security
against its enemies. I, for one, will not participate in this dangerous
and disingenuous tactic.

I plan to continue to oppose certain of the proposed reforms,
while seeking balanced compromises. At the same time, I plan to
increase my investments in Israel, because I trust it to resolve the
judicial reform dispute in a democratic and stable manner.

L. If You Truly Love Israel, It's Time to Compromise

The Knesset has just enacted a law prohibiting the Supreme Court
from striking down legislative and administrative decisions on the
grounds that they are "unreasonable." No other country in the world
permits its Supreme Court such broad authority.

Most require a violation of the constitution to strike down laws
or actions by the other branches, but Israel has no written constitution, so the Supreme Court has arrogated to itself this unusual power.

Reasonable people could disagree about whether unelected
judges should or should not have the authority to strike down the
actions of other branches based on an open-ended criterion such as
unreasonableness. In general, I would think that courts should not
have such untrammeled authority.

But Israel may be different because it has a unicameral legislature
and no written constitution, so the Supreme Court serves as the only
real institutional check on the excesses of the other branches.

Of course, the ultimate check in Israel, as in any democracy, is
elections. Israel has many of those, perhaps too many, as evidenced

by the handful it has had in as many years. But even elections cannot change the composition of the Supreme Court, whose justices serve subject only to an age restriction.

This debate over the concept of reasonableness is an appropriate subject for discussion and peaceful protest. It is not, in my view, a justification for the refusal of military reservists to perform their duty, for doctors to strike, or for protesters to engage in civil disobedience. But these extreme measures are not merely a response to the recent law; they grow out of fear that this is only the first push down a slippery slope—a slope that will end with a substantial weakening of the judicial branch, and especially of the controversial Supreme Court.

On a broader level, it is also a protest against the entire current Israeli government headed by Prime Minister Benjamin Netanyahu, that includes several reactionary extremists from the religious and nationalistic hard right. But this government was elected by the people, albeit in an extremely close vote, followed by the cobbling together of Israel's first coalition that included such extremist elements.

Protesters claim that this judicial reform, especially if followed by further weakening of the Supreme Court, will end Israeli democracy. They are categorically wrong. As President Isaac Herzog told a combined session of the US Congress, democracy is in Israel's DNA, and it will remain there forever. The best proof that this is true is both the frequency of Israeli elections and the intensity of the recent protests on both sides. These are not symptoms of a weakening of democracy; they are evidences of a strong democracy at work.

The most disturbing aspect of this controversy is that it has become internationalized. Judicial reform is a domestic issue, whether in the United States, in India, or in Israel. Other countries should butt out of this entirely domestic issue. It does not affect the United States, Great Britain, the European Union, or the United Nations.

But Israel has always been subjected to a double standard of scrutiny with regard to its domestic concerns. This internationalization of a purely domestic issue is partly a result of that double standard, but it is also the responsibility of some of the Israeli protesters who have sought help from outside the country. In doing so, they are deliberately weakening the Israeli economy, just as the refusal of soldiers to serve is weakening Israel's military capacity.

The extremes on both sides of this debate are overreacting and harming Israel in the process. The controversy over judicial reform requires moderate compromises from both sides.

Those who love Israel, whether inside or outside the nation-state of the Jewish people, must pull back from extreme measures and advocacy and follow President Isaac Herzog's lead in seeking a compromise that is acceptable, even if not preferred, by the majority of Israelis who favor a middle ground.

M. Why Biden Might Be the Dems' Last Pro-Israel President

Long-range planners in Israel worry Joe Biden may be the last pro-Israel Democratic president.

More fundamentally, they fear Israel is quickly becoming a wedge issue separating Democrats from Republicans. Backing for the nation-state of the Jewish people has historically been bipartisan, with Democrats being slightly more supportive. But this has changed recently for several reasons.

First, Israel has moved more to the right as the result of demographic changes: increased immigration from former Communist countries and higher birth rates among ultra-Orthodox and Sephardic Jews. And the refusal of Palestinian leaders to accept peace proposals has weakened the left.

Second, the Republican Party, especially its influential evangelical base, has become more supportive of Israel than old-line business-oriented Republicans used to be.

Finally, and most important, younger Democrats are moving to the left (and away from the increasingly conservative Israeli government). And their decreasing support for Israel is not necessarily limited to the current regime. It may represent a fundamental turn toward the Palestinian narrative, which emphasizes "anti-colonialism" and other mantras of the left.

This shift away from bipartisan backing has not yet been felt on the ground. Military and intelligence cooperation between the two nations is as strong as it has ever been. With a few exceptions, so is diplomatic cooperation. But domestic political support among elected Democratic offcials has wavered of late.

This reflects the ambivalence among many Democratic voters about Israel, with recent polls showing increasingly favorable attitudes toward the Palestinian side by younger Democrats, including young Jews. The growing influence of the rabidly anti-Israel radical wing of the Democratic Party may portend the future. It will certainly have an effect on the primaries, where a relatively small but energized group can determine the outcome—as evidenced by the 2018 primary victory of Alexandria Ocasio-Cortez in a heavily Democratic New York district.

We will likely see more such victories by radical anti-Israel Democrats in years to come. [This is now occurring as a result of the events of October 7 and the reactions to it.]

The diminishing support for Israel among the Democratic Party's left wing coupled with the expanding support among Republicans has not yet had a discernable impact on American Jews, who still vote overwhelmingly for Democrats. That's because Israel is less central to Jewish voters' identity than it used to be. [This may have changed after October 7.] Other issues—such as choice, the environment, gay and transgender rights, gun control, separation of church from state—are at least equally important. Indeed, Israel is more important to many Christian evangelicals than to some Reform and Conservative Jews.

Candidates reflect the views of voters, so our fear that Biden ends up the last Democratic candidate for president who strongly supports Israel may well prove accurate. If so, Israel will become even more of a wedge issue, especially since all likely Republican candidates in 2024 and beyond are certain to continue Donald Trump's vigorous advocacy. That wedge is evident already in several European countries, where the government's support for Israel depends on whether the right or left wins.

Israel must prepare itself for that eventuality here as well. It cannot count on pressure by American Jewish voters, most of whom are likely to continue to vote Democrat even if that party turns away from Israel.

Things may change, of course. If Israel were to become involved in a hot war with Iran that posed an existential threat, many more Jewish voters might prioritize their support.[3] If the Israeli government were to move more toward the center, some voters could view it more favorably.

The same might be true if a deal were made with the Palestinians. But no one can count on any such changes. The likely future is a growing wedge between the Democrats and Republicans over Israel. This poses a dilemma for longtime Democrats who do prioritize backing for Israel. Should we remain within the Democratic Party and try to influence it away from its shift against Israel? Or should we give up on the party we have supported for so long and help the party now on the Israel side of the wedge?

I am planning to remain a Democrat and vote for Biden while seeking to marginalize the radical anti-Israel elements in that party.

N. Elon Musk Is Right About George Soros—and Not Anti-Semitic

Elon Musk has been accused of anti-Semitism because of his criticism and mockery of George Soros. Mr. Soros is Jewish; Mr. Musk isn't. But Mr. Musk stands falsely accused. Mr. Soros is an active participant in politics, and his Jewishness shouldn't shield him from criticism.

Further, no single person has done more to damage Israel's standing in the world, especially among so-called progressives, than George Soros. His financial support has multiplied the influence of the two major organizations that have done the most to shift the left-wing paradigm against Israel.

One of them is Human Rights Watch, which was founded by publisher and human-rights advocate Robert Bernstein (1923–2019). For years HRW critiqued the denial of human rights by all countries based on two criteria: the seriousness of the violations in any particular nation, and the inability of the nation's citizens to protest and remedy such violations. But in 1993 Kenneth Roth

---

3   This was written before the recent war in Gaza, which changed these dynamics.

became executive director and turned HRW into an organization that specialized in demonizing Israel.

By 2009 the Israel bashing had become so severe that Bernstein wrote: "As the founder of Human Rights Watch, its active chairman for twenty years and now founding chairman emeritus, I must do something that I never anticipated: I must publicly join the group's critics. Human Rights Watch had as its original mission to pry open closed societies, advocate basic freedoms, and support dissenters. But recently it has been issuing reports on the Israeli-Arab conflict that are helping those who wish to turn Israel into a pariah state."

Mr. Roth has deployed "human rights" as a weapon against Israel. His organization's one-sided reports were used to justify selective condemnation of Israel by the United Nations and its divisions. They were circulated on university campuses around the world. Despite their obvious anti-Israel bias, supporters pointed to Mr. Roth's Jewish heritage to lend credibility to his anti-Israel accusations.

"Here is an organization created by the goodwill of the free world to fight violations of human rights, which has become a tool in the hands of dictatorial regimes to fight against democracies," observed Natan Sharansky, the former Soviet dissident and Israeli Knesset member, in 2009. "It is time to call a spade a spade. The real activity of this organization today is a far cry from what it was set up thirty years ago to do: throw light in dark places where there is really no other way to find out what is happening regarding human rights."

In 2010, Mr. Soros said he planned to give $100 million, "the largest gift by far that Human Rights Watch has ever received," the *New York Times* reported. The paper quoted Mr. Soros: "Every Wednesday morning at 8 o'clock, a group at Human Rights Watch got together and discussed issues with the managers," he said. "I was an active participant in that group, and human rights remains an important element of my foundation's current activities."

The other organization is J Street. Despite its claim to be a progressive pro-Israel and pro-Palestinian organization, J Street has done much to turn most progressive and some liberal Democrats—including members of Congress, academics, and media figures—against Israel. Last year *Haaretz* reported that Mr. Soros contributed

$1 million to J Street's super PAC, "20 times larger than any previous donation J Street Action Fund received."

I'm not the only Jewish American to criticize Mr. Soros. In a January article for the Jewish News Service, Farley Weiss, a former president of the National Council of Young Israel, wrote: "Soros's defenders try to shut down criticism of the billionaire by claiming it is anti-Semitic because Soros himself is Jewish. But no one has financed more destructive attacks on Israel and the American Jewish community than Soros."

Mr. Soros also has had a pernicious influence on American domestic issues, such as funding leftist candidates for district attorney, who have politicized law enforcement. Unlike Mr. Musk, I haven't compared Mr. Soros to Magneto, a Marvel supervillain who, like Mr. Soros, survived the Holocaust. I wouldn't make that comparison because I had never heard of Magneto. But I agree with Mr. Musk that Mr. Soros's acts contribute to fraying the "fabric of civilization." And Mr. Musk has shown no hostility toward Israel or the Jewish people.

Some right-wing anti-Semites have focused on Mr. Soros in promoting conspiracy theories about "the Jews" controlling the world. Critics of Mr. Soros should join supporters in condemning such misuse of his Jewish heritage. But this misuse shouldn't deter legitimate criticism of the malign influence Mr. Soros has on the world—irrespective of his being Jewish.

O. Taxpayers Shouldn't Foot the Bill for CUNY Law's Official Anti-Semitism

What would the reaction be if a publicly funded law school offcially endorsed the candidacy of Donald Trump? Or offcially supported white supremacy? Or invited as graduation speaker an overtly anti-gay bigot? Would defenders of such action claim free speech? Or would they admit there is a difference between an individual expressing bigoted views and a state-sponsored institution offcially endorsing such hateful positions?

That is the question posed, in reverse, by recent actions taken on behalf of the taxpayer-funded City University of New York School of Law. That law school, part of the system where I attended college

(Brooklyn College), has become the hotbed of anti-Americanism, anti-Zionism, and anti-Semitism.

For at least two years now, the offcial graduation speaker, selected by the students and approved by the administration, has used the occasion to spout some of the most rabid hate speech against the American military, the American police, the Israeli army, and the Israeli people.

This year's speaker, Fatima Mohammed, called the police and the army "fascists." She railed against the people of Israel and the nation-state of the Jewish people. School offcials, including Dean Sudha Setty, applauded as Mohammed spat venom out at the May 12 ceremony. Nor was this an isolated situation.

The faculty as a whole has endorsed the boycott movement against Israel, which is anti-Semitic to the core. It prohibits any contact between American academics and Jewish academics in Israel and calls for Israel's end, demanding it be replaced by a Palestinian state, "from the river to the sea," which includes Tel Aviv, Haifa, Jerusalem and all the rest of Israel.

Imagine being a CUNY Law student who supports Israel's right to exist. His or her belief is offcially contradicted by the faculty, whose responsibility includes grading and recommending students. It is wrong for a law school, especially one funded by taxpayers, to formally endorse such hatred against the Jewish citizens of Israel.

On a recent CUNY group chat, anti-Semites were warned not to shout "F–k the Jews" but instead to substitute "Zionists" for "Jews," although the meaning remains clear. Indeed, one of the people on the chat then tweeted "F–k all the Jews." This reflects the feeling of many at CUNY Law and many of those who vigorously applauded the speaker's vicious anti-Semitic vitriol.

The City University of New York law school should become a private institution and no longer receive public funds unless it ceases to be the academic loudspeaker for anti-Americanism, anti-Zionism, and anti-Semitism.

This year's graduation speaker described the law itself as "a manifestation of white supremacy" and called for "revolution" against the legal system. She praised CUNY Law as the only institution that reflects her hatred.

New York City and state taxpayers should not be required to pay for this institutionalized hate speech. Let the marketplace of ideas prevail and let students who agree with Fatima Mohammed's view of American law and Jews attend a private law school that advocates such hatred without governmental financial support.

The government has no obligation or indeed legitimate right to lend its imprimatur to ideologically driven bigotry. Cutting off government financing may help return CUNY's law school to its proper mission of teaching students how to think about the law instead of propagandizing the students about who to hate.

CUNY Law is an embarrassment to the city university system. It is not a credible place of learning. It is a propaganda mill for radical anti-American and anti-Israel students who should have the right to a real legal education that will prepare them to practice law rather than to spew hatred and foment revolution.

No one should try to prevent Fatima Mohammed from exercising her constitutional right to spread falsehoods about America, Israel, or Jews. But she has no right to have her hate speech receive the imprimatur of our government and the financial support of citizens who disagree with her bigotry.

The situation does not pass the shoe-on-the-other-foot test: No reasonable person would support a taxpayer institution that offcially espoused hated against African American or Arab-American students. Yet that is exactly what CUNY Law is doing against patriotic American, Zionist, and Jewish students, alumni, and all decent people. This double standard should not be accepted.

P. Why Have So Many Neo-Nazis Rallied to Ukraine's Cause?

Brave Ukrainian soldiers are risking their lives to defend their nation and their families against Russian aggression. There's only one problem: many of those fighting for today's Ukraine also seem to be fighting for a Ukrainian past that is shameful.

Most Americans and Europeans applaud the heroic Ukrainian military and hope for its victory over Russia's aggression. But these same people might restrain their clapping if they knew how many of these Ukrainian and allied "heroes" are wearing symbols that are unambiguously associated with Hitler's Nazi Germany.

Some of the most recent battles of the war have taken place inside Russia itself, with the border city of Belgorod coming under attack by a group of volunteers who bring nothing but discredit to Ukrainian President Volodymyr Zelenskyy's government. The Russian Volunteer Corps is run by Denis Kapustin, who openly espouses Hitler's views.

But such ideology and symbology are not confined to Ukraine's allied forces. Rather, they are to be found in many places on the Ukrainian sides of the front lines.

A group called the Azov Brigade fought bravely to defend eastern Ukraine, holding out in Mariupol's Azovstal Steel Plant for weeks after others had given up hope. Unfortunately, the same Azov Brigade has proudly boasted of its neo-Nazi ideology and wore their own version of the swastika until it was no longer convenient for them to do so. Yet the unit has been "folded into Ukrainian military" and become an important component of it.

Among the symbols used by these neo-Nazi groups is the "Totenkopf," the death's head worn by extermination camp guards and others who perpetrated the Holocaust. They also wear the black sun symbol, which is closely connected to Heinrich Himmler, the notorious head of the Nazi stormtroopers.

These symbols are associated not only with Nazism and anti-Semitism but with white supremacy and anti-gay groups.

The *New York Times* has described the relationship between Ukraine and Nazi imagery as "complicated." If that is somehow intended as a justification, it defies history. Although many Ukrainians were killed by German soldiers, too many also joined with the German military in its genocidal program. The SS organized a subgroup in Ukraine called the 14th SS-Volunteer Division "Galicia." Many Ukrainian Nazis volunteered to become death camp guards in Poland, and many were complicit in the massacre of Jews at Babi Yar. A considerable number of Ukrainians supported the Nazi invasion of their country and saw it as liberating them from the oppression of the Soviet Union. That was then! But there is no excuse or justification for the current Ukrainian leadership tolerating the glorification of the Nazis and the widespread and open use of Nazi symbols by its soldiers.

Historically, Ukraine has been one of the most anti-Semitic countries in the world. Even before the Nazi invasion, Ukrainian citizens conducted pogroms and mass killings of Jews. One of the worst offenders was Bohdan Khmelnytsky, who several hundred years ago murdered tens of thousands of Jewish women, babies, and men, in a prelude to the Holocaust, and in the name of Ukrainian nationalism. That, too, was then, but now the statue of this anti-Semitic mass murderer stands proudly at the center of Kyiv and his picture adorns current Ukrainian currency.

So, the issue is not complex. There are still far too many Ukrainian anti-Semites and neo-Nazis. This presents a problem not only for the current war with Russia, but also for its aftermath. If the Ukrainian military defeats Russia, many of these Nazis will be regarded as heroes. Some will almost certainly be elected to positions of power and authority. If Ukraine loses the war to Russia, these neo-Nazis will surely blame it on the Jews and on the Jewish president of Ukraine. As is often the case when extremism is tolerated, it becomes a lose-lose proposition for the Jews.

The *New York Times* points out that some Russian soldiers also wear Nazi symbols, as if that somehow justifies the actions of the neo-Nazis on the side of "good." It only goes to show that anti-Jewish racism (a better term than anti-Semitism) is pervasive both on the extreme right and the extreme left, among ultra-nationalists and anti-nationalists and on both sides of the Ukrainian-Russian war. Whatever other variables there may be, the one constant over the millennia has been the "blame the Jews" trope.

The *Times* reports that even some Jewish organizations are prepared to give Ukraine a pass on its toleration of neo-Nazis, because they don't want to be perceived as supporting Russian President Vladimir Putin's narrative about Ukraine being a Nazi state. Ukraine is not a Nazi state; it is a state that elected a Jew as president, while tolerating Nazism in its military. Those who refuse to condemn such intolerable toleration only encourage it by their mistaken silence.

Calling out military groups that would like to turn Ukraine into a Nazi state, does not further the Russian narrative. It only tells a painful truth about the present, the past, and the likely future.

Q. Allies Did Not Punish Nazi Germany Enough

Hitler said getting rid of the Jews would lead to prosperity and the West fulfilled that promise.

The successful emergence of Germany from the horrors it inflicted during WWII cannot be denied. But neither should the moral costs of that success be denied. The Marshall Plan, which rebuilt and enriched West Germany, helped it become the showcase of capitalism in the face of the Eastern communism of the Soviet Union and the countries it controlled, including East Germany. Part of the reason why the Berlin Wall came down and Russian communism ended was the more affluent lives being lived by the citizens of those nations that were not under Soviet control. The Marshall Plan worked as it was intended to.

But what about the moral costs of enriching West Germany and its people so soon after the Holocaust? Hitler told the Germans that if they got rid of the Jews, they would prosper. The Marshall Plan made that lethal prediction come true for West Germans (and for East Germans as well, following the unification). Perhaps it was a moral cost worth incurring, in light of the positive outcome for democracy. But it was a significant, indeed incalculable, cost that has rarely been acknowledged.

Immanuel Kant would have recognized the moral cost of rewarding Germany, and so many of its hands-on Nazi mass murderers, in order to achieve the important goal of winning the Cold War. Kant famously argued that punishment for past serious crimes like murder must be deemed an end unto itself, not a means of achieving future benefits. To illustrate the absoluteness of this categoric imperative, he devised the following hypothetical: "Even if a civil society were to dissolve itself by common agreement, the last murderer remaining in prison must first be executed."

Most people would agree that this extreme example takes the principle too far. There must be room for compassion, rehabilitation, and important future considerations. But many would also agree that the imperative of punishing serious crimes must be given considerable weight in any moral calculus. Even those who would give it less weight should be troubled by any result that rewards, rather than punishes, past criminality in order to promote future goals.

A balance must be struck between the moral imperative of punishing (and not rewarding) past crimes and the pragmatic needs of promoting future benefits, such as defeating totalitarianism. The critical question, therefore, is whether the postwar response to Nazi atrocities—the Marshall Plan coupled with the trials of individual Nazi war criminals—struck the proper balance. I think it did not. Too many Nazis and collaborators lived too good lives, unrepentant for their horrible crimes. Too few were punished or even condemned. Too many companies that worked slaves to their deaths were back in business too quickly and too profitably.

The so-called Morgenthau Plan, which would have denied Germany the resources to once again become an industrial power, was opposed by many as too harsh. Some thought it wasn't harsh enough. The aging President Roosevelt put it this way: "There are two schools of thought—those who would be altruistic in regard to the Germans, hoping by loving kindness to make them Christians again, and those who would adopt a much tougher attitude. Most decidedly, I belong to the latter school, for though I am not blood-thirsty, I want the Germans to know that this time at least, they have definitely lost the war." After Roosevelt died, the mood shifted toward strengthening West Germany. Hence, the Marshall Plan.

I recall a class I taught in the late 1960s that included several McCloy fellows who were from German universities. (Ironically, John McCloy was America's high commissioner to occupied West Germany who pardoned many war criminals and returned assets to criminal companies.) I asked whether knowing everything they now know about Germany between 1933 and the late 1960s, would they have joined the Nazi party in 1933? Most said no. I then asked them to put aside moral considerations and do a simple cost-benefit calculation based only on pragmatic considerations. The students were split down the middle. I wonder how many citizens of West Germany would honestly admit that knowledge of the future Marshall Plan would have influenced their decision whether to vote for Hitler in 1933.

The Marshall Plan is merely a powerful example of the larger philosophical question debated by Kant, Bentham, and their followers: how much weight to accord the moral imperatives of punishing past criminality and how much to accord the pragmatic claims of the future. These issues were front and center following the Rwandan genocide and South African apartheid. They are part of an even broader debate between the absolute moral imperatives of the Kantian schools that include Jesuit and other religious thinkers on the one hand, and the alleged moral relativism of the pragmatic utilitarian schools of Bentham, Mill and Dewey, on the other. This debate is most consequential when it involves issues of life and death, as it surely does in the context of the Holocaust and "never again."

R. ICC Must Investigate Russians for War Crimes—and Ukrainians, If Warranted

The United States government has now offcially accused Russia of war crimes.

President Joe Biden declared in his address in Warsaw, Poland, that Russia had committed "crimes against humanity." Although his announcement has no legal import, it may well encourage the International Criminal Court (ICC) to move more aggressively.

There can be no doubt that as a matter of international law, Russia is committing war crimes against the Ukrainian people.

Deliberately targeting civilians is a war crime. So is killing a number of civilians, even if not specifically targeted, that is disproportionate to the legitimate military value of the target.

The evidence is clear that Russia is committing both of these categories of criminal behavior. These crimes do not, in my view, qualify as "genocide"—the worst crime of all—but they do meet the standards for crimes against humanity. The crimes of which they have been accused justify investigation and likely prosecution by appropriate international tribunals, as well as by nations whose courts claim universal jurisdiction over such crimes.

The remaining question is whether such tribunals exist and, if so, whether they are willing and able to bring perpetrators to justice. Neither Russia nor Ukraine (nor the US) is a signatory to the Rome Treaty that established the ICC, though Ukraine has submitted to its jurisdiction. But the ICC claims the power to investigate and prosecute all war criminals, without regard to the country they belong to, if they can secure personal jurisdiction over them.

The court has no jurisdiction over nations, only individuals. There are ongoing efforts therefore to identify specific Russian individuals who are responsible for war crimes. If they are identified, arrest warrants can be issued, and if they are arrested, they can be brought to The Hague and placed on trial. Obviously, the perpetrators include high-ranking Russian offcials, including President Vladimir Putin, as well as several generals. It is highly unlikely, however, that these criminals will leave the safety of Russia, Belarus, or other nations that will not allow their arrest. Moreover, diplomatic immunity poses barriers to arrest.

Nonetheless, it would be important for the prosecutors in The Hague to conduct criminal investigations and issue warrants for anyone against whom the evidence the evidence supports arrests. Even if only symbolic, criminal warrants might well have some deterrent impact on culpable lower-ranking Russian soldiers and civilians who may someday want to travel beyond the safety of their home country.

Accordingly, the ICC prosecutor's offce should establish (if it has not already done so) a task force designed to gather and evaluate all available evidence of war crimes.

The focus should be on Russian actions, but if there is evidence of any Ukrainian war crimes by specific soldiers or others, they, too, must be investigated and, if warranted, prosecuted. War crimes know no uniforms or nations. They are individual, as well as collective.

Unfortunately, war crimes are committed in virtually all protracted military conflicts. And the term *war crimes* has been weaponized by all sides and thrown around so promiscuously as to lose much of its meaning and moral force. It is being selectively applied (and ignored) by the United Nations institutions, by non-governmental organizations (NGOs) such as Amnesty International, and by some media.

But what Russian forces have done and allegedly continue to do—targeting apartment buildings, murdering civilians with hands tied behind their backs, raping women—is so clearly criminal that these actions must be prosecuted if the prohibition against war crimes is to retain any credibility.

Much of the evidence of war crimes is already publicly available from video footage and eyewitness accounts. Russians have offered no defense beyond the usual "they are doing it too."

This excuse will suffce neither in an actual court or the court of public opinion.

There is the risk, of course, that if Putin is indicted—even if he cannot be arrested—he will escalate his criminal behavior, because he has nothing further to fear from the courts. But this danger should not deter the ICC from doing its job: identifying, investigating, indicting, and, where possible, prosecuting war criminals, regardless of their status or position.

So let the investigations commence. Let the warrants issue. And let the process of justice commence, even if it will never be satisfactorily completed.

S. Rabbis Should Not Protest Israel at the UN

A group of reform and conservative rabbis protested against Israel in front of the UN on the day Israel's prime minister represented the nation-state of the Jewish people. They claimed that their protest was directed against Israel's duly elected prime minister, Benjamin Netanyahu, for his government's support of judicial reform—which has divided the Israeli people. But let there be no mistake about it: this protest is seen by Israel's enemies—and there are plenty of them at the UN—as an attack against Israel by American Jews.

It would be different if the protests took place in front of the Israeli embassy or consulate or even in front of the hotel where Netanyahu is staying, as some are scheduled to take place. But the UN is the central locus of hatred against Israel, which is condemned by the General Assembly and other bodies more frequently than all the other nations of the world combined. The nation-state of the Jewish people is accused—and convicted—of apartheid, genocide, ethnic cleansing, and being undemocratic, while other nations that are actually guilty of these crimes and sins are given a pass. These rabbis give credibility to those blood libels against Israel by falsely claiming that the proposed judicial reforms will end democracy in Israel. I do not recall them protesting at the UN against the Palestinian leader for claiming that Hitler murdered Jews because they were money lenders, or Iranian Holocaust deniers, or the many anti-democratic Arab and Muslim leaders. Their anger is directed only at the one nation that is singled out for double standard condemnation by the UN.

First, the claims by the rabbis are categorically false, reflecting an abysmal ignorance of the role of judicial review in Western democracies governed by the rule of law. I am personally opposed to most of the proposed reforms, and if I were asked to vote either yes or no on the package as a whole, I would vote no. I believe that Israel is better off with today's imperfect system of judicial review than with the even less good proposed reforms. But that yes or no decision is not the only, or even most likely, option. Compromise is possible, and Israel's excellent president, Isaac Herzog, is working tirelessly to achieve a compromise that moderates on both sides can live with. But extremists are both sides are rejecting reasonable compromises because they are benefiting from the protests and counterprotests that strengthen their bases. The provocative and divisive protests at the UN will make compromise even more difficult.

I have been studying, teaching, litigating, and writing about judicial review for more than sixty years. I can state—and I challenge anyone to dispute this—that the current Israel Supreme Court is the most powerful in the democratic world. No other court—including in the US, Great Britain, and other Western democracies—can overrule legislative or executive decisions based on lawsuits brought by ordinary citizens who are not individually harmed by these decisions. Other courts require what is known as "standing" to bring "cases and controversies." Other courts do not strike down the decisions of duly elected and appointed executive officers on the grounds of unreasonableness, even extreme unreasonableness. They leave it to elected officials to decide what is reasonable in a democracy.

Israel will remain among the handful of the most democratic nations in the UN regardless of how the controversy over judicial reform plays out, because it will be resolved by democratic processes. This includes the weekly protests, which have generally been models of organized objections to controversial government policies, especially as compared to France, the US, and other democracies. The decision about judicial reform will and should be made by Israeli citizens, not by American rabbis, complaining to Israel's enemies at the UN about a complex issue regarding the role of the Israeli Supreme Court in the governance of its citizens.

T. Zelenskyy Emerges as Serious, Smart, Pragmatic—and Understandably Worried about American Backing for Ukraine

I had the privilege of meeting with President Zelenskyy and his chief of staff, who were in the United States to garner support for their defensive military actions against Russia. They were concerned about diminishing enthusiasm among some American voters for the expensive aid—both military and financial—that our nation has been giving the beleaguered Ukrainians.

I met with Mr. Zelenskyy at a hotel suite near the UN. He was being interviewed by my friend Greta Van Susteren for a Newsmax program. The owner of Newsmax, Christopher Ruddy, invited me to ask the president and his chief of staff some questions off camera. He was on the way to Washington, to make his case to America's leaders.

I told him that my family came from Galicia, part of which is now Ukraine, and that I had represented one of his predecessors, Leonid Kuchma, in a criminal case in Kiev. We discussed continuing

American support for his country's brave defense of their homeland. I found him to be serious, responsive, smart, pragmatic—and understandably worried.

In our deeply divided country, few issues are nonpartisan. Support for Ukraine should be one of them. There are politicians in both parties who oppose support for Ukraine, but the vast majority of Democrats and Republicans understand that if Russia is allowed to secure territory, and control the people therein, by aggressive and unprovoked military action, this will encourage President Putin as well as other tyrants to continue to violate international law.

There are legitimate criticisms of Ukraine, as there are of virtually every embattled country in the world. Ultra-nationalistic elements within Ukraine's armed forces display symbols that have long been associated with Nazism. Ukraine's record during the Holocaust was praised by Mr. Zelenskyy, though he should know better because he himself lost relatives during the Holocaust and many Ukrainians supported the Nazi genocide against the Jews.

There are still symbols of anti-Semitism throughout Ukraine, most disturbingly the statue at Kiev of the Cossack leader, Bogdan Chmelnitzki, who massacred thousands of Jews in the seventeenth century. His picture is still featured on Ukrainian currency. It is remarkable that in the face of this lingering bigotry, the Ukrainian people voted for a president who is openly Jewish.

Despite its blemished past, Ukraine now deserves support from our nation to prevent the unjustified targeting of civilians by Mr. Putin's armed forces. Recall that Russia, too, has a deeply blemished past when it comes to bigotry, but more importantly it has an unacceptable present, when it comes to, among other issues, military aggression.

There are many other nations in the world with aggressive ambitions. Among them is Communist China, which has set its sights on capturing and occupying the democratically governed island of Taiwan. Iran, too, has ambitions beyond its borders, as evidenced by its virtual occupation of Lebanon and its determination to obtain a nuclear arsenal.

Although America is not, and should not be, the policeman of the world, it is in America's best interest to use its power and influence to deter the ambitions of rogue nations.

Ukraine's greatest fear is that support for its defensive actions will become a partisan issue in the 2024 presidential election. President Biden has thus far given considerable, though not unlimited, support to Ukraine. Some influential Republicans, however, want to challenge this support in the upcoming election.

They cite polls showing diminished enthusiasm among some American voters for the vast expenditures of funds needed to support a faraway nation. Mr. Zelenskyy wants to keep Ukraine out of the upcoming US election. He wants support for Ukraine to be bipartisan, especially between the candidates.

Mr. Zelenskyy is correct about his concerns. Although it is in the interest of all Americans to deny Mr. Putin an unlawful and immoral victory, Ukraine is not a high-priority issue among many voters. It is in the nature of today's politics that when one side strongly supports an issue, the other side looks for opportunities to exploit the division among voters to their partisan advantage.

Yet the future of Ukraine and international stability is too important to become a divisive partisan issue. All Americans should stand against Mr. Putin's unjustified aggression. So should the rest of the international community, because while today Ukraine is the target—tomorrow Russian aggression may be coming to a theater near you.

U. My Dinner with Netanyahu

When I attended Prime Minister Netanyahu's speech at the UN, he and his wife invited me and my wife to join them and some friends for Shabbat dinner. The PM asked me to sit next to him and we spent the next three hours discussing and debating the proposed judicial reform and other issues dividing Israel and their supporters around the world.

The previous evening, I spoke at a rally in support of Israeli democracy, which I said would endure even if all the judicial reforms— many of which in their current form I do not support—were to be enacted. Counterdemonstrators across the street, who claim to support democracy, tried to shout me down and to prevent me from making the case for compromise. They reminded me of the woke students who try to shout down speakers with whom they disagree, all in the supposed name of what they regard as democracy:

Free speech for me but not for thee.

My discussions with Netanyahu—whom I've known for more than a half-century—centered around the controversial proposals to curtail the power of the Supreme Court and to give politicians more of a role in selecting justices. The prime minister indicated a willingness to negotiate compromises on some of the disputed provisions but said that extremists on the other side refused to budge, because they believed they were strengthening their base by conducting protests both in Israel and in the US. To my mind, he seemed eminently reasonable—far more so than he is portrayed by protesters and much of the media. I offered my help in trying to broker a compromise, since I have friends on both sides of the issue.

The president of Israel, Isaac Herzog, is also interested in facilitating compromise, but extremists on both sides seem to prefer division to unity. I believe that the vast majority of Israelis would approve reasonable compromises, but the extremists who oppose a negotiated resolution are louder and more belligerent than the centrists.

Very few of those who protested Bibi at the UN—including reform and conservative rabbis_have any real understanding of the issues involved in the proposed reforms. They simply don't like Netanyahu and the coalition he was forced to assemble in order to cobble together a governing majority.

The reality is that the current Israel Supreme Court is the most powerful in the word. Its power to strike down laws enacted, and actions taken, by the elected branches of government exceeds that of any other democracy. There is no requirement that a litigant must have "standing": thus, majority laws and actions can be challenged by anyone. There is no prohibition on the court entering into the thicket of politics or the complexities of economics: thus, the court can second guess political and economic decisions. Until a recent law was enacted by the Knesset, the Supreme Court could strike down executive auctions that a majority of the justices deemed "unreasonable." The US Supreme Court has no such powers. Nor do the high courts of other democracies.

Netanyahu justifies the reforms he supports by saying he wants to make Israel's Supreme Court more like ours and the courts in other democracies. And I believe him. But some on the extreme right of his coalition want to politicize the courts in their direction and weaken its power to overrule the majority. They also want to control the selection process by which judges are appointed. Many opponents of any reform want to hand Netanyahu a political defeat and destroy his coalition, without regard to the merits or demerits of specific proposals. Netanyahu himself seeks a compromise that defuses the deep divisions in the country while allowing the current coalition to survive or be expanded.

One thing is clear to me, based both on my discussions with Netanyahu and my considerable knowledge of the Israeli legal system: The proposed reforms have nothing to do with helping the prime minister defend himself against the criminal charges he is currently facing. These charges are quite weak and may well fail on their own merits and demerits. Moreover, the specific reforms have little or no impact on the ongoing trial.

Considering all the pressures, both domestic and international, that Bibi is under, he was remarkably upbeat, optimistic, and even funny during our dinner. He is one of the smartest, best educated, hardworking, and perceptive leaders in the world. And it shows both in private and public. [One week later, everything changed with the Hamas attack of October 7.]

Alan Dershowitz and Cornel West Debate on Fox—October 12, 2023[1]

Sean Hannity: 2024 presidential candidate, former Harvard professor Cornel West, said the students were largely right but they lacked nuance. He joins us now with reaction, along with attorney, also Harvard professor Alan Dershowitz is with us. Thank you both for being with us.

I would usually—you always call me Brother Sean, I call you Brother Cornel. I'm not—I'm not that happy with you tonight.

Because we have thirty-one groups from Harvard. Harvard's supposed to be_I always thought the top of the top, to get into Harvard, what a—what an accomplishment, what an achievement, what academic excellence you must show, a cut above everyone else, and thirty-one student groups blaming Israel, blaming the victim.

And your answer to this is they are largely right? Hamas that murdered children, Hamas that murdered innocent people.

West: Read the rest of what I said though, brother . . .

Hannity: They are largely right but lacking nuance.

West: The words were that Israel's policies of war crimes and collective punishment against Palestinian set of context . . .

---

1   Slightly edited to avoid repetition.

West: And Hamas must take responsibility for killing innocent people. Anybody who kills innocent people is engaging in barbaric acts.

Hannity: You said Israel—and the United States are primarily responsible—

West: The United States has supported and enabled this—

Hannity: You explain to this audience . . . how is Israel and the United States responsible for beheading forty children? How?

West: I'm talking about the context. Five hundred and forty-five Palestinian children died in August 2004, not one American said a word. I believe a Palestinian baby has the same value as an Israeli baby. So when you have that kind of vicious hatred and revenge, you get response of hatred and revenge.

They are all wrong. They're all war crimes. They're all to be condemned, but you cannot simply look at this particular moment without the larger backdrop of an ugly occupation and the ugly attacks chronically against Palestinian.

Professor Dershowitz?

Alan Dershowitz: I complained when Palestinian children were killed, but I explained the concept of why they were killed. Here is one of the leaders of Hamas.

"For the Palestinian people, death has become an industry. The elderly excel at this and so do the children. This is why we have formed human shields of the women and the children."

Hamas is the one responsible for the killing of Palestinian children. Also, Hamas has a term, it's called the CNN strategy, which is to induce Israel into killing Palestinian children by using them as human shields, then parade the bodies out on CNN, and you'll see what happens, people like Cornel West will engage in crocodile tears, blame it on Israel when the entire blame is on Hamas for using their children as human shields and then using their children as shields—

West: I have the same outrage when Palestinian babies are killed, when Jewish babies or Israeli babies.

Dershowitz: It shouldn't be the same outrage.

West: I want you to have the same indignation when Palestinians are killed.

Dershowitz: Not when they're killed . . . by Palestinians. You can't make a moral comparison: When Nazi kids were killed in the bombings of Dresden, I wouldn't have the same compassion as when Jewish kids were put in gas chambers and crematoriums.

You're a professor of theology, don't you understand the moral difference between deliberately murdering a kid and having collateral damage because they're human shields? You're running for President of the United States, what would you do . . . if terrorists were firing at American children in America and the terrorists were hiding behind Palestinian children? Would you allow the killing of Americans to continue, or would you go and get the terrorists even if it meant possibly collateral damage on Palestinians? What would you do?

West: I'll tell you exactly what I would do. First, truth and morality tend to be two casualties in any context of war. I would want to tell the American people the truth. I would tell them what the context is, how we found ourselves in this situation.

Hannity: You're not answering the question—

West: I would not jump for a military invasion and a genocidal attack on a—

Dershowitz: A genocidal attack?

West: On Gaza.

Dershowitz: No, no, it's not a genocidal attack.

West: This is like Warsaw 1943. Where do they go?

Dershowitz: Let me tell you where they go. They go to the UN, which has safe places in Gaza. They go to the Rafah crossing—

West: Eleven UN people have been killed in the last few days.

Dershowitz: They go to Egypt.

West: Egypt—they can't get out? Come on, brother.

Dershowitz: Let me make another thing clear. Gaza City is very dense.

West: Absolutely, it's dense.

Dershowitz: But Gaza itself, the Gaza Strip, there's lots of room. The Israelis have said, get out of Gaza City, go to Rafah, go to Khan Yunis, go to other places. And you know what Hamas is saying?

West: But no water, no food, no electricity, all in the dark?

Dershowitz: You know what Hamas is saying? Hamas is saying don't go.

West: I'm not here to defend Hamas. I'm not defending Hamas. You ever lie on me like that, brother. I'm defending the suffering and—of Palestinians. . . .

Hamas itself committed war crimes. Anybody who commits war crimes is barbaric. I'm saying that explicitly.

But I want you to say, if the Israeli Defense Forces are killing children, are they barbaric, too?

Dershowitz: No.

West: Are they ever barbaric?

Dershowitz: If they were to target children—

West: Have they ever targeted children?

Dershowitz: No.

West: Never ever—

Dershowitz: Never, in the history—

West: In seventy, eighty years.

Dershowitz: — have they ever targeted a child.

West: Oh, buddy, you got to get off the crack pipe.

Dershowitz: They never targeted a child.

West: They kill one innocent person—

Dershowitz: Not purposely, no.

West: To 1948—

Dershowitz: Not purposely.

West: Are they that pure? Are they that pristine? Come on, brother.

Dershowitz: You don't have to be very pure not to kill a child. Because they're being used as human shields.

Hannity: Let me show something we showed on this program last night. What I'm about to show this audience these are cartoons that are aired in Gaza for young children that are taught to hate the Jewish people. You just watch this for a second, and I'll have you both comment. Watch that. [Shows video of Hamas teaching children to hate Jews.]

Hannity: — if you brainwash and indoctrinate young children, that you're teaching them to hate from that young age, not good.

West: No. Any kind of inculcation of hatred is immoral and wrong.

Dershowitz: Would you condemn Black Lives Matter Chicago for justifying the Hamas murder by using these hang gliders and coming down on the music event?

West: I would certainly condemn it.

Dershowitz: You condemn Black Lives Matter?

West: I would condemn anybody, not a matter of skin.

Dershowitz: Okay, I'm glad to hear it.

West: This is morality and spirituality, my brother.

Dershowitz: Okay, so you condemn Black Lives Matter.

West: He asked me what I would do. I would say we've got to end occupation. We got to make sure that Palestinians have the same dignity, the same rights as Israelis.

Dershowitz: You know I support that. You know I support the two-state solution, but Hamas doesn't support two-state solution.

Hannity: Professor West, I want to ask this question. Would Gaza be facing annihilation if Hamas did not attack and kill all these innocent Israelis?

Dershowitz: Of course not.

West: Gaza has been facing—

Hannity: He's not answering. Would they be facing an imminent annihilation?

West: — this chronic process of annihilation since 2000—

Dershowitz: 2000 and what?

West: Since 2006 and '07, and Gaza was taken over by Hamas. I'm not pro-Hamas. I'm pro-democracy, but I'm concerned about the suffering of Palestinian folks.

Dershowitz: Israel didn't fire a single rocket until Hamas fired five thousand rockets.

West: Israel controls the land, the air—

Dershowitz: Only after Hamas took over.

West: — the food going in, the trade coming, and so forth. But it was already under occupation since 1967.

Dershowitz: No, the occupation ended 2005. Learn your history.

West: Oh.

Dershowitz: [Former prime minister Ariel] Sharon left every Israeli settler, every Israeli soldier left. In 2005–2006, it was like Singapore, it could have been the nicest place in the Mediterranean, then Hamas overthrew them—

West: You don't think New York would be under occupation if another country owned its air, its space, its food going in?

Dershowitz: It didn't own it between 2005 and 2007.

Hannity: Let me end with this, here's a sad fact, this debate could not be held on Harvard's campus today, correct?

Dershowitz: That's right. I would not be permitted to speak at Harvard in support of Israel.

Hannity: To go up to Harvard—I am offering to go up to Harvard and do, and I will moderate it.

West: We've debated before—

Hannity: I don't think Harvard will let Professor Dershowitz or Professor Brother Hannity debate on campus.

Dershowitz: You know what? If Harvard won't allow it, go to Columbia. They won't allow it either.

Hannity: I agree with you. We're going to ask them.

The Legal Context

Nitsana Darshan-Leitner: One of the most prominent lawyers in the US. Professor Dershowitz, thank you so much for joining us.

Professor Dershowitz: Well, it's a great honor. Yours is a wonderful organization, holding the enemies of freedom and justice to the rule of law is a very high calling. And you do it so well. I've been a big supporter of the organization from the very beginning.

Darshan-Leitner: Professor Dershowitz, many commentators demand that Israel act proportionally. What does it mean in this situation, in this current war? Is it even a principle which binds Israel?

Dershowitz: It is a principle, but the commentators don't have any understanding of it. What they think it means is that if a thousand rockets were sent to kill Israeli children, that Israel is only entitled to send a thousand rockets back at Hamas terrorists. That's not the principle of proportionality.

Under the principle of proportionality, Israel is allowed to win an overwhelming victory. If one rocket is sent, they're allowed to send a thousand rockets. If one Israeli soldier is killed, they're allowed to kill ten thousand Hamas soldiers. The principle of proportionality has nothing, nothing to do with proportional responses against the military or against terrorists. It means only one thing: if a military action is being planned, and you know there is a possibility of collateral civilian deaths or injuries, the value of the target selected, and the means selected must be proportional to the number of civilians that are going to be put in harm's way. In other words, if there's one terrorist hiding in a hospital, and you could kill that one terrorist by blowing up the hospital, no, proportionality doesn't allow that. But if you have a thousand terrorists hiding in an area with only a few civilians, then you can destroy the area even though you know you're going to be killing some civilians. The civilian deaths must be proportional to the value of the target.

Now, Israel's target in Gaza is the legitimate one—to destroy Hamas's complete military infrastructure and ability to fight back. That's a legitimate target, and Israel therefore can take actions that it knows will cause civilian deaths as long as it takes every precaution to try to minimize those civilian deaths. Israel's military goal is so important and so broad to prevent the recurrence of the killing of fourteen hundred innocent people, the taking of two hundred people as hostages. That is such an important military target that proportionality permits actions which they know may very well kill Palestinian civilians.

Dershowitz: Now we also understand what does it mean to be a Palestinian civilian? This is not like Berlin in 1945, where you had Nazi soldiers in uniforms, the Luftwaffe, or the SS, and you had perfectly innocent civilians. And yet, of course, the United States sieged the city, didn't let in any water, didn't let in any electricity. But it's very different. With Hamas, you don't know who a civilian is. About twenty years ago, I developed a concept called the continuum of civilianality. It starts with a three-year-old child. Nothing can be more civilian than a three-year-old child. But it moves along and says, what about a seventeen-year-old girl who helps load rockets into or allows his home to be used to harbor Hamas or to fire rockets? There's a continuum. And the closer you come to military part of the continuum, the more freedom Israel has to endanger the lives of so-called "civilians." But obviously, when you're dealing with children, babies, totally and completely innocent people, the rules are somewhat different.

So it's complex in Gaza. But so far, Israel has been complying not only with the letter, but with the spirit of proportionality and the other principle of distinction, distinction between civilians and military.

Darshan-Leitner: You said it's a complex situation and we have a lot of lawyers in the crowd but non-lawyers as well. And this is an asymmetrical war. So, can you explain what legal principles bind Israel in its fight against Hamas, which is a non-state? Just give us a background, how the international law binds Israel, what type of rules should apply.

Dershowitz: Again, they're very complex. Normally, combatants are treated differently than noncombatants. Sometimes they're treated more generously. For example, when a combatant is captured, they have to be treated as prisoner of war. They can't be tortured, they can't be put on trial, they can't be executed. But if a civilian engages in activities, they can be treated as criminals. They can be put on trial, they can be sentenced to any sentence that's permissible under law. And so, where you have people during the day, they're building houses or they're selling bread, but come four o'clock, they put on their green bandana and they start building rockets, they go on Saturday morning wearing a bandana to kill Israelis. They are treated in the worst possible way under the law. They're not prisoners of war. You can kill them because they're not part of official armed forces. They're not wearing official uniforms. They're not part of a military hierarchy. So you can treat them the way, for example, the United States treated Nazi spies when they caught them off the beach of Rockaway in the 1940s.

They did not treat them as prisoners of war. They tried them in a tribunal. They sentenced them to death, and they executed them. And so, Israel has the right to treat Hamas combatants in the worst possible way, either as prisoners of war or as civilian criminals. They can either use law enforcement tactics against them or military tactics against them. But the one thing they can't give them is any kind of exemption because they're not full-time military under the usual rules of law.

Darshan-Leitner: Let's talk about Hamas. Hamas operates by blending into the civilian population. Does the law give Israel some measure of lenience to act where Hamas's service do not distinguish themselves from civilians?

Dershowitz: Yes, of course. Now the hardest question is what about human shields? And we have videos of Hamas leaders saying our women and our children—we use them for human shields. If you use a woman or a child for a human shield, it really depends on whether or not they have consented to that. For example, family members of the leaders of Hamas who live with them. Israel has sent in rockets that have killed the leaders along with some of their family members. If on the other hand, the human shields are hostages, even though they're Palestinian hostages, much like the Israelis are hostages, then Israel has to take great care in trying to avoid casualties.

But remember one thing that's clear under international law. Israel is entitled to prefer the life of its own civilians to the life of Palestinian civilians. When there's a hard question, a hard decision, they are entitled to prefer the lives of their own civilians if there's a choice. They are surely entitled to prefer the lives of their own soldiers over Hamas soldiers. But in general, a nation is entitled to use self-defense, even if they know that there will be civilian casualties.

Let's remember too that Hamas makes it a policy of what they call the CNN strategy. They quite deliberately put civilians in harm's way in order for Israel to kill them so that they can take babies out and put them in front of TV cameras. Hamas calls that the CNN strategy. I call it the dead baby strategy. And Israel is entitled to respond to that in whatever way it chooses. That's not a moral legal question. That is a tactical question. The same is true of Israel's attempts to rescue its own hostages. There are no laws that govern that. These are Israel's own citizens and they have to make the judgment as to what risks to take with the hostages in order to rescue some of them or in order to achieve the other legitimate goals that they're seeking to achieve in Gaza.

Darshan-Leitner: Right. So one of the goals was, we saw it in the beginning of the war when Israel puts a siege over Gaza immediately the first day. Can Israel blockade Gaza?

Dershowitz: Of course.

Darshan-Leitner: Does Israel have a responsibility to provide water, electricity, food or medical care to Gaza? Is it even a blockade?

Dershowitz: The answer legally is no. They have no obligation. John Bolton, the former national security adviser to the President of the United States, made the point very well that when the United States blockaded Berlin, there was no obligation to send water or electricity, or when the United States blockaded other cities. Blockades and seizures are common under international law. Now, it would be good if Israel sent in minimum, minimum amounts of food rations, enough to keep the people alive, but not enough to make them happy, and gave them just enough water.

Remember, Israel provides only 8 percent of Gaza's water. So, Gaza has an obligation. to receive its water from other sources. We know for sure that the leaders of Hamas have [a] storehouse, lots of water, they have lots of generators, let them use their generators to give to hospitals instead of using them to send rockets.

Israel has no obligation to send in anything that in any way helps Hamas defeat Israel militarily. And so the answer is for the most part Israel is entitled to engage in a reasonable blockade, but it should do so, if it can, without compromising its military efficiency by not taking it out on pure, pure civilians by which I mean children.

And remember CNN always says half of Gaza's children. That's nonsense. First of all, the statistic is false. Number two: Is a sixteen-year-old who wears the Hamas headband and goes into Israel a child? Is a fifteen-year-old girl who's used as a human shield a child? No, of course not. If you're old enough to kill Israelis, you're not a child. And Israel is entitled to treat fifteen- and sixteen-year-olds the way they treat thirty-year-olds. And don't be fooled by the other phony statistic that Gaza is the most densely populated part of the world. I think it ranks sixty-third. Tel Aviv, New York, Manila are more densely populated—and there are open areas of Gaza. I've been there. I know you can walk into open fields, you can go to the south of Gaza. And if you have to live in a tent, if you have to live outdoors, fine. If only the Jews of the Holocaust had been given that option. The Palestinians have been given the option. They've been told to go South. And Hamas has said, no, die instead, be human shields, stay North. That's not the fault of Israel.

Darshan-Leitner: So, in your opinion, after the disengagement from 2006, when Israel disengaged from Gaza, does Israel have any responsibility for the civilian population in Gaza? The Supreme Court in Israel had an opinion about it, which concluded with having some responsibility, at least moral responsibility. Do you share a different opinion?

Dershowitz: I think it depends on when we're talking about it. We're talking about 2005, 2006, beginning of 2007, when there was no Israeli presence there and when the Palestinian Authority technically ruled the land and there were no blockades to speak of. Israel had no responsibility whatsoever. Once Hamas took over and they started sending in rockets and Israel controlled the airspace and controlled the entrance and exit. At that point when there was no state of war, they had a negative responsibility not to block access to food supplies but remember that Qatar claims to be sending food supplies to Gaza. But we know that Qatar is sending material that's used and was used in these raids. We know a lot of it comes from Iran. So, Israel has to put its own interests first.

Let me make one general point. Israel has made a terrible mistake over the past years in listening to international opinion, in paying attention to Human Rights Watch, in paying any attention to the United Nations. Israel has a much higher standard of morality than any of these organizations. The United States is different. The United States, of course, killed hundreds of thousands of civilians in Iraq and in Afghanistan. But Israel has no choice but to be lectured to by the United States because the United States provides it so much material support. But it need not listen to Great Britain. It need not listen to the European community. It need not listen to Human Rights Watch. Israel should never make a decision that endangers its own civilians or its own troops in order to placate or satisfy hypocritical double standard international opinion. Israel's morality is higher. It should use its own morality and it should always resolve doubts in favor of its own citizens and its own soldiers as every country in the world has done throughout history. The world cannot impose a double standard of morality on Israel.

(Applause)

Darshan-Leitner: Amazing.

(Applause)

Darshan-Leitner: And just lastly, while we have you on the stage, Professor Dershowitz, you remember the story with Harvard University. Since the war began, several Harvard student groups issued a statement in which Harvard students blamed Israel for rape, murder, and kidnapping of its own citizens. You know, can you give your take on this story?

Dershowitz: This is not surprising to me. During the 1930s, both Yale and Harvard students supported Hitler and Nazis. It was very common. Yale, more than Harvard, but Harvard too. Columbia supported Mussolini. Students tend to be extremists. They tend not to see the difference often between right and wrong. They have their own definition. Harvard has a long, long policy of discriminating against Jews.

There's a long article in the *New York Sun* which discloses the history of Harvard. I am currently ashamed to be associated with Harvard, which I have been associated with for sixty years. I and other Jewish professors helped make the reputation of Harvard and Harvard has turned its back on its Jewish faculty, on its Jewish students, on its Jewish administrators.

You know when George Floyd was killed, one Black man who was filled with drugs and had a long criminal record, but he was tragically murdered by the police, Harvard had their reckoning. It changed admission standards, it changed the curriculum, it looked to its history. It's about time Harvard does a reckoning with its problem relating to Jews.

In the 1930s Harvard gave honors to Nazis, Harvard administrators went over to celebrate the anniversary of a Nazi university. Harvard's history in relation to Jews included a short positive period, which happened to coincide with the period when I was there from

1964 say to the beginning of the twenty-first century. It was a golden era, but that has changed dramatically.

The new president of Harvard does not seem to have the same kind of sensitivities towards some of these issues. Yes, she spoke at Chabad the other night and said some of the right things, but she has refused to categorically make the following statement: "I condemn any student at Harvard who has shown any support for rapists, for murderers, for beheaders, and kidnappers. Those students do not belong at Harvard. We can't throw them out because they have a freedom of speech right, but I have a freedom of speech as president of Harvard to condemn in the strongest term these students." Until she says that, Harvard will be falling into a moral abyss and it has to have its own reckoning with its flawed history in relation to Jews, to Israel, and to a range of issues relating to the Jewish people and its nation state.

Darshan-Leitner: Well, thank you very much, Professor Dershowitz. Thank you for being the long-term supporter of the Jewish state, a defender of Israel . . .

Hamas Charter

The Covenant of the
Islamic Resistance Movement
18 August 1988

In the Name of the Most Merciful Allah

"Ye are the best nation that hath been raised up unto mankind: ye command that which is just, and ye forbid that which is unjust, and ye believe in Allah. And if they who have received the scriptures had believed, it had surely been the better for them: there are believers among them, but the greater part of them are transgressors. They shall not hurt you, unless with a slight hurt; and if they fight against you, they shall turn their backs to you, and they shall not be helped. They are smitten with vileness wheresoever they are found; unless they obtain security by entering into a treaty with Allah, and a treaty with men; and they draw on themselves indignation from Allah, and they are afflicted with poverty. This they suffer, because they disbelieved the signs of Allah, and slew the prophets unjustly; this, because they were rebellious, and transgressed." (Al-Imran—verses 109–111).

Israel will exist and will continue to exist until Islam will obliterate it, just as it obliterated others before it" (The Martyr, Imam Hassan al-Banna, of blessed memory).

"The Islamic world is on fire. Each of us should pour some water, no matter how little, to extinguish whatever one can without waiting for the others." (Sheikh Amjad al-Zahawi, of blessed memory).

In the Name of the Most Merciful Allah

Introduction

Praise be unto Allah, to whom we resort for help, and whose forgiveness, guidance and support we seek; Allah bless the Prophet and grant him salvation, his companions and supporters, and to those who carried out his message and adopted his laws—everlasting prayers and salvation as long as the earth and heaven will last. Hereafter:

O People:

Out of the midst of troubles and the sea of suffering, out of the palpitations of faithful hearts and cleansed arms; out of the sense of duty, and in response to Allah's command, the call has gone out rallying people together and making them follow the ways of Allah, leading them to have determined will in order to fulfill their role in life, to overcome all obstacles, and surmount the difficulties on the way. Constant preparation has continued and so has the readiness to sacrifice life and all that is precious for the sake of Allah.

Thus it was that the nucleus (of the movement) was formed and started to pave its way through the tempestuous sea of hopes and expectations, of wishes and yearnings, of troubles and obstacles, of pain and challenges, both inside and outside.

When the idea was ripe, the seed grew and the plant struck root in the soil of reality, away from passing emotions, and hateful haste. The Islamic Resistance Movement emerged to carry out its role through striving for the sake of its Creator, its arms intertwined with those of all the fighters for the liberation of Palestine. The spirits of its fighters meet with the spirits of all the fighters who have sacrificed their lives on the soil of Palestine, ever since it was conquered by the companions of the Prophet, Allah bless him and grant him salvation, and until this day.

This Covenant of the Islamic Resistance Movement (HAMAS), clarifies its picture, reveals its identity, outlines its stand, explains its aims, speaks about its hopes, and calls for its support, adoption and joining its ranks. Our struggle against the Jews is very great and very serious. It needs all sincere efforts. It is a step that inevitably should be followed by other steps. The Movement is but one squadron that should be supported by more and more squadrons from this vast Arab and Islamic world, until the enemy is vanquished and Allah's victory is realised.

Thus we see them coming on the horizon "and you shall learn about it hereafter" "Allah hath written, Verily I will prevail, and my apostles: for Allah is strong and mighty." (The Dispute—verse 21).

"Say to them, This is my way: I invite you to Allah, by an evident demonstration; both I and he who followeth me; and, praise be unto Allah! I am not an idolator." (Joseph—verse 107).

Hamas (means) *strength and bravery* -**(according to)**
Al-Mua'jam al-Wasit: c1.

Definition of the Movement
Ideological Starting-Points

[List of Articles follow]
Article One:
The Islamic Resistance Movement: The Movement's programme is Islam. From it, it draws its ideas, ways of thinking and understanding of the universe, life and man. It resorts to it for judgement in all its conduct, and it is inspired by it for guidance of its steps.

The Islamic Resistance Movement's Relation with the Moslem Brotherhood Group:
Article Two:
The Islamic Resistance Movement is one of the wings of Moslem Brotherhood in Palestine. Moslem Brotherhood Movement is a universal organization which constitutes the largest Islamic movement in modern times. It is characterised by its deep understanding, accurate comprehension and its complete embrace of all Islamic concepts of all aspects of life, culture, creed, politics, economics, education,

society, justice and judgement, the spreading of Islam, education, art, information, science of the occult and conversion to Islam.

Structure and Formation
Article Three:
The basic structure of the Islamic Resistance Movement consists of Moslems who have given their allegiance to Allah whom they truly worship,—"I have created the jinn and humans only for the purpose of worshipping"—who know their duty towards themselves, their families and country. In all that, they fear Allah and raise the banner of Jihad in the face of the oppressors, so that they would rid the land and the people of their uncleanliness, vileness and evils.

"But we will oppose truth to vanity, and it shall confound the same; and behold, it shall vanish away." (Prophets—verse 18).

Article Four:
The Islamic Resistance Movement welcomes every Moslem who embraces its faith, ideology, follows its programme, keeps its secrets, and wants to belong to its ranks and carry out the duty. Allah will certainly reward such one.

Time and Place Extent of the Islamic Resistance Movement
Article Five:
Time extent of the Islamic Resistance Movement: By adopting Islam as its way of life, the Movement goes back to the time of the birth of the Islamic message, of the righteous ancestor, for Allah is its target, the Prophet is its example and the Koran is its constitution. Its extent in place is anywhere that there are Moslems who embrace Islam as their way of life everywhere in the globe. This being so, it extends to the depth of the earth and reaches out to the heaven.

"Dost thou not see how Allah putteth forth a parable; representing a good word, as a good tree, whose root is firmly fixed in the earth, and whose branches reach unto heaven; which bringeth forth its fruit in all seasons, by the will of its Lord? Allah propoundeth parables unto men, that they may be instructed." (Abraham—verses 24–25).

Characteristics and Independence
Article Six:
The Islamic Resistance Movement is a distinguished Palestinian movement, whose allegiance is to Allah, and whose way of life is Islam. It strives to raise the banner of Allah over every inch of Palestine, for under the wing of Islam followers of all religions can coexist in security and safety where their lives, possessions and rights are concerned. In the absence of Islam, strife will be rife, oppression spreads, evil prevails and schisms and wars will break out.

How excellent was the Moslem poet, Mohamed Ikbal, when he wrote:

"If faith is lost, there is no security and there is no life for him who does not adhere to religion. He who accepts life without religion, has taken annihilation as his companion for life."

The Universality of the Islamic Resistance Movement:
Article Seven:
As a result of the fact that those Moslems who adhere to the ways of the Islamic Resistance Movement spread all over the world, rally support for it and its stands, strive towards enhancing its struggle, the Movement is a universal one. It is well-equipped for that because of the clarity of its ideology, the nobility of its aim and the loftiness of its objectives.

On this basis, the Movement should be viewed and evaluated, and its role be recognised. He who denies its right, evades supporting it and turns a blind eye to facts, whether intentionally or unintentionally, would awaken to see that events have overtaken him and with no logic to justify his attitude. One should certainly learn from past examples.

The injustice of next-of-kin is harder to bear than the smite of the Indian sword.

"We have also sent down unto thee the book of the Koran with truth, confirming that scripture which was revealed before it; and preserving the same safe from corruption. Judge therefore between them according to that which Allah hath revealed; and follow not their desires, by swerving from the truth which hath come unto thee. Unto every of you have we given a law, and an open path; and if Allah had pleased, he had surely made you one people; but he hath thought it fit to give you different laws, that he might try you in that which he hath given you respectively. Therefore strive to excel each other in good works; unto Allah shall ye all return, and then will he declare unto you that concerning which ye have disagreed." (The Table, verse 48).

The Islamic Resistance Movement is one of the links in the chain of the struggle against the Zionist invaders. It goes back to 1939, to the emergence of the martyr Izz al-Din al Kissam and his brethren the fighters, members of Moslem Brotherhood. It goes on to reach out and become one with another chain that includes the struggle of the Palestinians and Moslem Brotherhood in the 1948 war and the Jihad operations of the Moslem Brotherhood in 1968 and after.

Moreover, if the links have been distant from each other and if obstacles, placed by those who are the lackeys of Zionism in the way of the fighters obstructed the continuation of the struggle, the Islamic Resistance Movement aspires to the realisation of Allah's promise, no matter how long that should take. The Prophet, Allah bless him and grant him salvation, has said:

"The Day of Judgement will not come about until Moslems fight the Jews (killing the Jews), when the Jew will hide behind stones and trees. The stones and trees will say O Moslems, O Abdulla, there is a Jew behind me, come and kill him. Only the Gharkad tree, (evidently a certain kind of tree) would not do that because it is one of the trees of the Jews." (related by al-Bukhari and Moslem).

The Slogan of the Islamic Resistance Movement:
Article Eight:
Allah is its target, the Prophet is its model, the Koran its constitution: Jihad is its path and death for the sake of Allah is the loftiest of its wishes.

Objectives
Incentives and Objectives
Article Nine:
The Islamic Resistance Movement found itself at a time when Islam has disappeared from life. Thus rules shook, concepts were upset,

values changed and evil people took control, oppression and darkness prevailed, cowards became like tigers: homelands were usurped, people were scattered and were caused to wander all over the world, the state of justice disappeared and the state of falsehood replaced it. Nothing remained in its right place. Thus, when Islam is absent from the arena, everything changes. From this state of affairs the incentives are drawn.

As for the objectives: They are the fighting against the false, defeating it and vanquishing it so that justice could prevail, homelands be retrieved and from its mosques would the voice of the mu'azen emerge declaring the establishment of the state of Islam, so that people and things would return each to their right places and Allah is our helper.

". . . and if Allah had not prevented men, the one by the other, verily the earth had been corrupted: but Allah is beneficent towards his creatures." (The Cow—verse 251).

Article Ten:
As the Islamic Resistance Movement paves its way, it will back the oppressed and support the wronged with all its might. It will spare no effort to bring about justice and defeat injustice, in word and deed, in this place and everywhere it can reach and have influence therein.

Strategies and Methods
**Strategies of the Islamic Resistance Movement:
Palestine Is Islamic aqf**

Article Eleven:
The Islamic Resistance Movement believes that the land of Palestine is an Islamic Waqf consecrated for future Moslem generations until Judgement Day. It, or any part of it, should not be squandered: it, or any part of it, should not be given up. Neither a single Arab country nor all Arab countries, neither any king or president, nor all the kings and presidents, neither any organization nor all of them, be they Palestinian or Arab, possess the right to do that. Palestine is an Islamic Waqf land consecrated for Moslem generations until

Judgement Day. This being so, who could claim to have the right to represent Moslem generations till Judgement Day?

This is the law governing the land of Palestine in the Islamic Sharia (law) and the same goes for any land the Moslems have conquered by force, because during the times of (Islamic) conquests, the Moslems consecrated these lands to Moslem generations till the Day of Judgement.

It happened like this: When the leaders of the Islamic armies conquered Syria and Iraq, they sent to the Caliph of the Moslems, Umar bin-el-Khatab, asking for his advice concerning the conquered land—whether they should divide it among the soldiers, or leave it for its owners, or what? After consultations and discussions between the Caliph of the Moslems, Omar bin-el-Khatab and companions of the Prophet, Allah bless him and grant him salvation, it was decided that the land should be left with its owners who could benefit by its fruit. As for the real ownership of the land and the land itself, it should be consecrated for Moslem generations till Judgement Day. Those who are on the land, are there only to benefit from its fruit. This Waqf remains as long as earth and heaven remain. Any procedure in contradiction to Islamic Sharia, where Palestine is concerned, is null and void.

"Verily, this is a certain truth. Wherefore praise the name of thy Lord, the great Allah." (The Inevitable—verse 95).

Homeland and Nationalism from the Point of View of the Islamic Resistance Movement in Palestine
Article Twelve:
Nationalism, from the point of view of the Islamic Resistance Movement, is part of the religious creed. Nothing in nationalism is more significant or deeper than in the case when an enemy should tread Moslem land. Resisting and quelling the enemy become the individual duty of every Moslem, male or female. A woman can go out to fight the enemy without her husband's permission, and so does the slave: without his master's permission.

Nothing of the sort is to be found in any other regime. This is an undisputed fact. If other nationalist movements are connected with materialistic, human or regional causes, nationalism of the Islamic Resistance Movement has all these elements as well as the more important elements that give it soul and life. It is connected to the source of spirit and the granter of life, hoisting in the sky of the homeland the heavenly banner that joins earth and heaven with a strong bond.

If Moses comes and throws his staff, both witch and magic are annulled.

"Now is the right direction manifestly distinguished from deceit: whoever therefore shall deny Tagut, and believe in Allah, he shall surely take hold with a strong handle, which shall not be broken; Allah is he who heareth and seeth." (The Cow—Verse 256).

Peaceful Solutions, Initiatives and International Conferences
Article Thirteen:
Initiatives, and so-called peaceful solutions and international conferences, are in contradiction to the principles of the Islamic Resistance Movement. Abusing any part of Palestine is abuse directed against part of religion. Nationalism of the Islamic Resistance Movement is part of its religion. Its members have been fed on that. For the sake of hoisting the banner of Allah over their homeland they fight. "Allah will be prominent, but most people do not know."

Now and then the call goes out for the convening of an international conference to look for ways of solving the (Palestinian) question. Some accept, others reject the idea, for this or other reason, with one stipulation or more for consent to convening the conference and participating in it. Knowing the parties constituting the conference, their past and present attitudes towards Moslem problems, the Islamic Resistance Movement does not consider these conferences capable of realising the demands, restoring the rights or doing justice to the oppressed. These conferences are only ways of setting the infidels in the land of the Moslems as arbitraters. When did the infidels do justice to the believers?

"But the Jews will not be pleased with thee, neither the Christians, until thou follow their religion; say, The direction of Allah is the true direction. And verily if thou follow their desires, after the knowledge which hath been given thee, thou shalt find no patron or protector against Allah." (The Cow—verse 120).

There is no solution for the Palestinian question except through Jihad. Initiatives, proposals and international conferences are all a waste of time and vain endeavors. The Palestinian people know better than to consent to having their future, rights and fate toyed with. As in said in the honourable Hadith:

"The people of Syria are Allah's lash in His land. He wreaks His vengeance through them against whomsoever He wishes among His slaves It is unthinkable that those who are double-faced among them should prosper over the faithful. They will certainly die out of grief and desperation."

The Three Circles
Article Fourteen:

The question of the liberation of Palestine is bound to three circles: the Palestinian circle, the Arab circle and the Islamic circle. Each of these circles has its role in the struggle against Zionism. Each has its duties, and it is a horrible mistake and a sign of deep ignorance to overlook any of these circles. Palestine is an Islamic land which has the first of the two kiblahs (direction to which Moslems turn in praying), the third of the holy (Islamic) sanctuaries, and the point of departure for Mohamed's midnight journey to the seven heavens (i.e. Jerusalem).

"Praise be unto him who transported his servant by night, from the sacred temple of Mecca to the farther temple of Jerusalem, the circuit of which we have blessed, that we might show him some of our signs; for Allah is he who heareth, and seeth." (The Night-Journey—verse 1).

Since this is the case, liberation of Palestine is then an individual duty for very Moslem wherever he may be. On this basis, the problem should be viewed. This should be realised by every Moslem.

The day the problem is dealt with on this basis, when the three circles mobilize their capabilities, the present state of affairs will change and the day of liberation will come nearer.

"Verily ye are stronger than they, by reason of the terror cast into their breasts from Allah. This, because they are not people of prudence." (The Emigration—verse 13).

The Jihad for the Liberation of Palestine is an Individual Duty
Article Fifteen:
The day that enemies usurp part of Moslem land, Jihad becomes the individual duty of every Moslem. In face of the Jews' usurpation of Palestine, it is compulsory that the banner of Jihad be raised. To do this requires the diffusion of Islamic consciousness among the masses, both on the regional, Arab and Islamic levels. It is necessary to instill the spirit of Jihad in the heart of the nation so that they would confront the enemies and join the ranks of the fighters.

It is necessary that scientists, educators and teachers, information and media people, as well as the educated masses, especially the youth and sheikhs of the Islamic movements, should take part in the operation of awakening (the masses). It is important that basic changes be made in the school curriculum, to cleanse it of the traces of ideological invasion that affected it as a result of the orientalists and missionaries who infiltrated the region following the defeat of the Crusaders at the hands of Salah el-Din (Saladin). The Crusaders realised that it was impossible to defeat the Moslems without first having ideological invasion pave the way by upsetting their thoughts, disfiguring their heritage and violating their ideals. Only then could they invade with soldiers. This, in its turn, paved the way for the imperialistic invasion that made Allenby declare on entering Jerusalem: "Only now have the Crusades ended." General Guru stood at Salah el-Din's grave and said: "We have returned, O Salah el-Din." Imperialism has helped towards the strengthening of ideological invasion, deepening, and still does, its roots. All this has paved the way towards the loss of Palestine.

It is necessary to instill in the minds of the Moslem generations that the Palestinian problem is a religious problem, and should be dealt with on this basis. Palestine contains Islamic holy sites. In it there is al-Aqsa Mosque which is bound to the great Mosque in Mecca in an inseparable bond as long as heaven and earth speak of Isra`

(Mohammed's midnight journey to the seven heavens) and Mi'raj (Mohammed's ascension to the seven heavens from Jerusalem).

"The bond of one day for the sake of Allah is better than the world and whatever there is on it. The place of one's whip in Paradise is far better than the world and whatever there is on it. A worshipper's going and coming in the service of Allah is better than the world and whatever there is on it." (As related by al-Bukhari, Moslem, al-Tarmdhi and Ibn Maja).

"I swear by the holder of Mohammed's soul that I would like to invade and be killed for the sake of Allah, then invade and be killed, and then invade again and be killed." (As related by al-Bukhari and Moslem).

The Education of the Generations
Article Sixteen:

It is necessary to follow Islamic orientation in educating the Islamic generations in our region by teaching the religious duties, comprehensive study of the Koran, the study of the Prophet's Sunna (his sayings and doings), and learning about Islamic history and heritage from their authentic sources. This should be done by specialised and learned people, using a curriculum that would healthily form the thoughts and faith of the Moslem student. Side by side with this, a comprehensive study of the enemy, his human and financial capabilities, learning about his points of weakness and strength, and getting to know the forces supporting and helping him, should also be included. Also, it is important to be acquainted with the current events, to follow what is new and to study the analysis and commentaries made of these events. Planning for the present and future, studying every trend appearing, is a must so that the fighting Moslem would live knowing his aim, objective and his way in the midst of what is going on around him.

"O my son, verily every matter, whether good or bad, though it be the weight of a grain of mustard-seed, and be hidden in a rock, or in the heavens, or in the earth, Allah will bring the same to light; for Allah is clear-sighted and knowing. O my son, be constant at prayer, and command that which is just, and forbid that which is evil: and be patient under the afflictions which shall befall thee; for this is a duty absolutely incumbent on all men. Distort not thy face out of contempt to men, neither walk in the earth with insolence; for Allah loveth no arrogant, vain-glorious person." (Lokman—verses 16–18).

The Role of the Moslem Woman
Article Seventeen:
The Moslem woman has a role no less important than that of the moslem man in the battle of liberation. She is the maker of men. Her role in guiding and educating the new generations is great. The enemies have realised the importance of her role. They consider that if they are able to direct and bring her up they way they wish, far from Islam, they would have won the battle. That is why you find them giving these attempts constant attention through information campaigns, films, and the school curriculum, using for that purpose their lackeys who are infiltrated through Zionist organizations under various names and shapes, such as Freemasons, Rotary Clubs, espionage groups and others, which are all nothing more than cells of subversion and saboteurs. These organizations have ample resources that enable them to play their role in societies for the purpose of achieving the Zionist targets and to deepen the concepts that would serve the enemy. These organizations operate in the absence of Islam and its estrangement among its people. The Islamic peoples should perform their role in confronting the conspiracies of these saboteurs. The day Islam is in control of guiding the affairs of life, these organizations, hostile to humanity and Islam, will be obliterated.

Article Eighteen:
Woman in the home of the fighting family, whether she is a mother or a sister, plays the most important role in looking after the family, rearing the children and embuing them with moral values and thoughts derived from Islam. She has to teach them to perform the religious duties in preparation for the role of fighting awaiting them. That is why it is necessary to pay great attention to schools and the curriculum followed in educating Moslem girls, so that they

would grow up to be good mothers, aware of their role in the battle of liberation.

She has to be of sufficient knowledge and understanding where the performance of housekeeping matters are concerned, because economy and avoidance of waste of the family budget, is one of the requirements for the ability to continue moving forward in the difficult conditions surrounding us. She should put before her eyes the fact that the money available to her is just like blood which should never flow except through the veins so that both children and grown-ups could continue to live.

"Verily, the Moslems of either sex, and the true believers of either sex, and the devout men, and the devout women, and the men of veracity, and the women of veracity, and the patient men, and the patient women, and the humble men, and the humble women, and the alms-givers of either sex who remember Allah frequently; for them hath Allah prepared forgiveness and a great reward." (The Confederates—verse 25).

The Role of Islamic Art in the Battle of Liberation
Article Nineteen:
Art has regulations and measures by which it can be determined whether it is Islamic or pre-Islamic (Jahili) art. The issues of Islamic liberation are in need of Islamic art that would take the spirit high, without raising one side of human nature above the other, but rather raise all of them harmoniously an in equilibrium.

Man is a unique and wonderful creature, made out of a handful of clay and a breath from Allah. Islamic art addresses man on this basis, while pre-Islamic art addresses the body giving preference to the clay component in it.

The book, the article, the bulletin, the sermon, the thesis, the popular poem, the poetic ode, the song, the play and others, contain the characteristics of Islamic art, then these are among the requirements of ideological mobilization, renewed food for the journey and recreation for the soul. The road is long and suffering is plenty. The soul will be bored, but Islamic art renews the energies, resurrects the movement, arousing in them lofty meanings and proper conduct.

"Nothing can improve the self if it is in retreat except shifting from one mood to another."

All this is utterly serious and no jest, for those who are fighters do not jest.

Social Mutual Responsibility

Article Twenty:

Moslem society is a mutually responsible society. The Prophet, prayers and greetings be unto him, said: "Blessed are the generous, whether they were in town or on a journey, who have collected all that they had and shared it equally among themselves."

The Islamic spirit is what should prevail in every Moslem society. The society that confronts a vicious enemy which acts in a way similar to Nazism, making no differentiation between man and woman, between children and old people—such a society is entitled to this Islamic spirit. Our enemy relies on the methods of collective punishment. He has deprived people of their homeland and properties, pursued them in their places of exile and gathering, breaking bones, shooting at women, children and old people, with or without a reason. The enemy has opened detention camps where thousands and thousands of people are thrown and kept under sub-human conditions. Added to this, are the demolition of houses, rendering children orphans, meting cruel sentences against thousands of young people, and causing them to spend the best years of their lives in the dungeons of prisons.

In their Nazi treatment, the Jews made no exception for women or children. Their policy of striking fear in the heart is meant for all. They attack people where their breadwinning is concerned, extorting their money and threatening their honour. They deal with people as if they were the worst war criminals. Deportation from the homeland is a kind of murder.

To counter these deeds, it is necessary that social mutual responsibility should prevail among the people. The enemy should be faced by the people as a single body which if one member of it should complain, the rest of the body would respond by feeling the same pains.

Article Twenty-One:

Mutual social responsibility means extending assistance, financial or moral, to all those who are in need and joining in the execution of some of the work. Members of the Islamic Resistance Movement should consider the interests of the masses as their own personal interests. They must spare no effort in achieving and preserving them. They must prevent any foul play with the future of the upcoming generations and anything that could cause loss to society. The masses are part of them and they are part of the masses. Their strength is theirs, and their future is theirs. Members of the Islamic Resistance Movement should share the people's joy and grief, adopt the demands of the public and whatever means by which they could be realised. The day that such a spirit prevails, brotherliness would deepen, cooperation, sympathy and unity will be enhanced and the ranks will be solidified to confront the enemies.

Supportive Forces Behind the Enemy
Article Twenty-Two:

For a long time, the enemies have been planning, skillfully and with precision, for the achievement of what they have attained. They took into consideration the causes affecting the current of events. They strived to amass great and substantive material wealth which they devoted to the realisation of their dream. With their money, they took control of the world media, news agencies, the press, publishing houses, broadcasting stations, and others. With their money they stirred revolutions in various parts of the world with the purpose of achieving their interests and reaping the fruit therein. They were behind the French Revolution, the Communist revolution and most of the revolutions we heard and hear about, here and there. With their money they formed secret societies, such as Freemasons, Rotary Clubs, the Lions and others in different parts of the world for the purpose of sabotaging societies and achieving Zionist interests. With their money they were able to control imperialistic countries and instigate them to colonize many countries in order to enable them to exploit their resources and spread corruption there.

You may speak as much as you want about regional and world wars. They were behind World War I, when they were able to destroy the Islamic Caliphate, making financial gains and controlling resources. They obtained the Balfour Declaration, formed the League of Nations through which they could rule the world. They were behind World War II, through which they made huge financial gains by trading in armaments, and paved the way for the establishment of their state. It was they who instigated the replacement of the League of Nations with the United Nations and the Security Council to enable them to rule the world through them. There is no war going on anywhere, without having their finger in it.

"So often as they shall kindle a fire for war, Allah shall extinguish it; and they shall set their minds to act corruptly in the earth, but Allah loveth not the corrupt doers." (The Table—verse 64).

The imperialistic forces in the Capitalist West and Communist East, support the enemy with all their might, in money and in men. These forces take turns in doing that. The day Islam appears, the forces of infidelity would unite to challenge it, for the infidels are of one nation.

"O true believers, contract not an intimate friendship with any besides yourselves: they will not fail to corrupt you. They wish for that which may cause you to perish: their hatred hath already appeared from out of their mouths; but what their breasts conceal is yet more inveterate. We have already shown you signs of their ill will towards you, if ye understand." (The Family of Imran—verse 118).

It is not in vain that the verse is ended with Allah's words "if ye understand."

Our Attitudes Towards:
A. Islamic Movements
Article Twenty-Three:
The Islamic Resistance Movement views other Islamic movements with respect and appreciation. If it were at variance with them on one point or opinion, it is in agreement with them on other points and understandings. It considers these movements, if they reveal good intentions and dedication to Allah, that they fall into the category

of those who are trying hard since they act within the Islamic circle. Each active person has his share.

The Islamic Resistance Movement considers all these movements as a fund for itself. It prays to Allah for guidance and directions for all and it spares no effort to keep the banner of unity raised, ever striving for its realisation in accordance with the Koran and the Prophet's directives.

"And cleave all of you unto the covenant of Allah, and depart not from it, and remember the favour of Allah towards you: since ye were enemies, and he reconciled your hearts, and ye became companions and brethren by his favour: and ye were on the brink of a pit of fire, and he delivered you thence. Allah declareth unto you his signs, that ye may be directed." (The Family of Imran—Verse 102).

Article Twenty-Four:
The Islamic Resistance Movement does not allow slandering or speaking ill of individuals or groups, for the believer does not indulge in such malpractices. It is necessary to differentiate between this behaviour and the stands taken by certain individuals and groups. Whenever those stands are erroneous, the Islamic Resistance Movement preserves the right to expound the error and to warn against it. It will strive to show the right path and to judge the case in question with objectivity. Wise conduct is indeed the target of the believer who follows it wherever he discerns it.

"Allah loveth not the speaking ill of anyone in public, unless he who is injured call for assistance; and Allah heareth and knoweth: whether ye publish a good action, or conceal it, or forgive evil, verily Allah is gracious and powerful." (Women—verses 147–148).

B. Nationalist Movements in the Palestinian Arena
Article Twenty-Five:
The Islamic Resistance Movement respects these movements and appreciates their circumstances and the conditions surrounding and affecting them. It encourages them as long as they do not give their allegiance to the Communist East or the Crusading West. It confirms

to all those who are integrated in it, or sympathetic towards it, that the Islamic Resistance Movement is a fighting movement that has a moral and enlightened look of life and the way it should cooperate with the other (movements). It detests opportunism and desires only the good of people, individuals and groups alike. It does not seek material gains, personal fame, nor does it look for a reward from others. It works with its own resources and whatever is at its disposal "and prepare for them whatever force you can", for the fulfilment of the duty, and the earning of Allah's favour. It has no other desire than that.

The Movement assures all the nationalist trends operating in the Palestinian arena for the liberation of Palestine, that it is there for their support and assistance. It will never be more than that, both in words and deeds, now and in the future. It is there to bring together and not to divide, to preserve and not to squander, to unify and not to throw asunder. It evaluates every good word, sincere effort and good offices. It closes the door in the face of side disagreements and does not lend an ear to rumours and slanders, while at the same time fully realising the right for self-defence.

Anything contrary or contradictory to these trends, is a lie disseminated by enemies or their lackeys for the purpose of sowing confusion, disrupting the ranks and occupy them with side issues.

"O true believers, if a wicked man come unto you with a tale, inquire strictly into the truth thereof; lest ye hurt people through ignorance, and afterwards repent of what ye have done." (The Inner Apartments—verse 6).

Article Twenty-Six:
In viewing the Palestinian nationalist movements that give allegiance neither to the East nor the West, in this positive way, the Islamic Resistance Movement does not refrain from discussing new situations on the regional or international levels where the Palestinian question is concerned. It does that in such an objective manner revealing the extent of how much it is in harmony or contradiction with the national interests in the light of the Islamic point of view.

C. The Palestinian Liberation Organization
Article Twenty-Seven:
The Palestinian Liberation Organization is the closest to the heart of the Islamic Resistance Movement. It contains the father and the brother, the next of kin and the friend. The Moslem does not estrange himself from his father, brother, next of kin or friend. Our homeland is one, our situation is one, our fate is one and the enemy is a joint enemy to all of us.

Because of the situations surrounding the formation of the Organization, of the ideological confusion prevailing in the Arab world as a result of the ideological invasion under whose influence the Arab world has fallen since the defeat of the Crusaders and which was, and still is, intensified through orientalists, missionaries and imperialists, the Organization adopted the idea of the secular state. And that it how we view it.

Secularism completely contradicts religious ideology. Attitudes, conduct and decisions stem from ideologies.

That is why, with all our appreciation for The Palestinian Liberation Organization—and what it can develop into—and without belittling its role in the Arab-Israeli conflict, we are unable to exchange the present or future Islamic Palestine with the secular idea. The Islamic nature of Palestine is part of our religion and whoever takes his religion lightly is a loser.

"Who will be adverse to the religion of Abraham, but he whose mind is infatuated? (The Cow—verse 130).

The day The Palestinian Liberation Organization adopts Islam as its way of life, we will become its soldiers, and fuel for its fire that will burn the enemies.

Until such a day, and we pray to Allah that it will be soon, the Islamic Resistance Movement's stand towards the PLO is that of the son towards his father, the brother towards his brother, and the relative to relative, suffers his pain and supports him in confronting the enemies, wishing him to be wise and well-guided.

"Stand by your brother, for he who is brotherless is like the fighter who goes to battle without arms. One's cousin is the wing one flies with—could the bird fly without wings?"

D. Arab and Islamic Countries
Article Twenty-Eight:
The Zionist invasion is a vicious invasion. It does not refrain from resorting to all methods, using all evil and contemptible ways to achieve its end. It relies greatly in its infiltration and espionage operations on the secret organizations it gave rise to, such as the Freemasons, The Rotary and Lions clubs, and other sabotage groups. All these organizations, whether secret or open, work in the interest of Zionism and according to its instructions. They aim at undermining societies, destroying values, corrupting consciences, deteriorating character and annihilating Islam. It is behind the drug trade and alcoholism in all its kinds so as to facilitate its control and expansion.

Arab countries surrounding Israel are asked to open their borders before the fighters from among the Arab and Islamic nations so that they could consolidate their efforts with those of their Moslem brethren in Palestine.

As for the other Arab and Islamic countries, they are asked to facilitate the movement of the fighters from and to it, and this is the least thing they could do.

We should not forget to remind every Moslem that when the Jews conquered the Holy City in 1967, they stood on the threshold of the Aqsa Mosque and proclaimed that "Mohammed is dead, and his descendants are all women."

Israel, Judaism and Jews challenge Islam and the Moslem people. "May the cowards never sleep."

E. Nationalist and Religious Groupings, Institutions, Intellectuals, the Arab and Islamic World
Article Twenty-Nine:
The Islamic Resistance Movement hopes that all these groupings will side with it in all spheres, would support it, adopt its stand and solidify its activities and moves, work towards rallying support for it so that the Islamic people will be a base and a stay for it, supplying it with strategic depth an all human material and informative spheres, in time and in place. This should be done through the convening of solidarity conferences, the issuing of explanatory

bulletins, favourable articles and booklets, enlightening the masses regarding the Palestinian issue, clarifying what confronts it and the conspiracies woven around it. They should mobilize the Islamic nations, ideologically, educationally and culturally, so that these peoples would be equipped to perform their role in the decisive battle of liberation, just as they did when they vanquished the Crusaders and the Tatars and saved human civilization. Indeed, that is not difficult for Allah.

"Allah hath written, Verily I will prevail, and my apostles: for Allah is strong and mighty." (The Dispute—verse 21).

Article Thirty:
Writers, intellectuals, media people, orators, educaters and teachers, and all the various sectors in the Arab and Islamic world—all of them are called upon to perform their role, and to fulfill their duty, because of the ferocity of the Zionist offensive and the Zionist influence in many countries exercised through financial and media control, as well as the consequences that all this lead to in the greater part of the world.

Jihad is not confined to the carrying of arms and the confrontation of the enemy. The effective word, the good article, the useful book, support and solidarity—together with the presence of sincere purpose for the hoisting of Allah's banner higher and higher—all these are elements of the Jihad for Allah's sake.

"Whosoever mobilises a fighter for the sake of Allah is himself a fighter. Whosoever supports the relatives of a fighter, he himself is a fighter." (related by al-Bukhari, Moslem, Abu-Dawood and al-Tarmadhi).

F. Followers of Other Religions: The Islamic Resistance Movement Is a Humanistic Movement
Article Thirty-One:
The Islamic Resistance Movement is a humanistic movement. It takes care of human rights and is guided by Islamic tolerance when dealing with the followers of other religions. It does not antagonize anyone of them except if it is antagonized by it or stands in its way to hamper its moves and waste its efforts.

Under the wing of Islam, it is possible for the followers of the three religions—Islam, Christianity and Judaism—to coexist in peace and quiet with each other. Peace and quiet would not be possible except under the wing of Islam. Past and present history are the best witness to that.

It is the duty of the followers of other religions to stop disputing the sovereignty of Islam in this region, because the day these followers should take over there will be nothing but carnage, displacement and terror. Everyone of them is at variance with his fellow-religionists, not to speak about followers of other religionists. Past and present history are full of examples to prove this fact.

"They will not fight against you in a body, except in fenced towns, or from behind walls. Their strength in war among themselves is great: thou thinkest them to be united; but their hearts are divided. This, because they are people who do not understand." (The Emigration—verse 14).

Islam confers upon everyone his legitimate rights. Islam prevents the incursion on other people's rights. The Zionist Nazi activities against our people will not last for long. "For the state of injustice lasts but one day, while the state of justice lasts till Doomsday."

"As to those who have not borne arms against you on account of religion, nor turned you out of your dwellings, Allah forbiddeth you not to deal kindly with them, and to behave justly towards them; for Allah loveth those who act justly." (The Tried—verse 8).

The Attempt to Isolate the Palestinian People
Article Thirty-Two:
World Zionism, together with imperialistic powers, try through a studied plan and an intelligent strategy to remove one Arab state after another from the circle of struggle against Zionism, in order to have it finally face the Palestinian people only. Egypt was, to a great extent, removed from the circle of the struggle, through the treacherous Camp David Agreement. They are trying to draw other Arab countries into similar agreements and to bring them outside the circle of struggle.

The Islamic Resistance Movement calls on Arab and Islamic nations to take up the line of serious and persevering action to prevent the success of this horrendous plan, to warn the people of the danger eminating from leaving the circle of struggle against Zionism. Today it is Palestine, tomorrow it will be one country or another. The Zionist plan is limitless. After Palestine, the Zionists aspire to expand from the Nile to the Euphrates. When they will have digested the region they overtook, they will aspire to further expansion, and so on. Their plan is embodied in the "Protocols of the Elders of Zion," and their present conduct is the best proof of what we are saying.

Leaving the circle of struggle with Zionism is high treason, and cursed be he who does that. "for whoso shall turn his back unto them on that day, unless he turneth aside to fight, or retreateth to another party of the faithful, shall draw on himself the indignation of Allah, and his abode shall be hell; an ill journey shall it be thither." (The Spoils—verse 16). There is no way out except by concentrating all powers and energies to face this Nazi, vicious Tatar invasion. The alternative is loss of one's country, the dispersion of citizens, the spread of vice on earth and the destruction of religious values. Let every person know that he is responsible before Allah, for "the doer of the slightest good deed is rewarded in like, and the does of the slightest evil deed is also rewarded in like."

The Islamic Resistance Movement consider itself to be the spearhead of the circle of struggle with world Zionism and a step on the road. The Movement adds its efforts to the efforts of all those who are active in the Palestinian arena. Arab and Islamic Peoples should augment by further steps on their part; Islamic groupings all over the Arab world should also do the same, since all of these are the best-equipped for the future role in the fight with the warmongering Jews.

". . . and we have put enmity and hatred between them, until the day of resurrection. So often as they shall kindle a fire of war, Allah shall extinguish it; and they shall set their minds to act corruptly in the earth, but Allah loveth not the corrupt doers." (The Table— verse 64).

Article Thirty-Three:

The Islamic Resistance Movement, being based on the common coordinated and interdependent conceptions of the laws of the universe, and flowing in the stream of destiny in confronting and fighting the enemies in defence of the Moslems and Islamic civilization and sacred sites, the first among which is the Aqsa Mosque, urges the Arab and Islamic peoples, their governments, popular and official groupings, to fear Allah where their view of the Islamic Resistance Movement and their dealings with it are concerned. They should back and support it, as Allah wants them to, extending to it more and more funds till Allah's purpose is achieved when ranks will close up, fighters join other fighters and masses everywhere in the Islamic world will come forward in response to the call of duty while loudly proclaiming: Hail to Jihad. Their cry will reach the heavens and will go on being resounded until liberation is achieved, the invaders vanquished and Allah's victory comes about.

"And Allah will certainly assist him who shall be on his side: for Allah is strong and mighty." (The Pilgrimage—verse 40).

The Testimony of History
Across History in Confronting the Invaders:
Article Thirty-Four:

Palestine is the navel of the globe and the crossroad of the continents. Since the dawn of history, it has been the target of expansionists. The Prophet, Allah bless him and grant him salvation, had himself pointed to this fact in the noble Hadith in which he called on his honourable companion, Ma'adh ben-Jabal, saying: O Ma'ath, Allah throw open before you, when I am gone, Syria, from Al-Arish to the Euphrates. Its men, women and slaves will stay firmly there till the Day of Judgement. Whoever of you should choose one of the Syrian shores, or the Holy Land, he will be in constant struggle till the Day of Judgement."

Expansionists have more than once put their eye on Palestine which they attacked with their armies to fulfill their designs on it. Thus it was that the Crusaders came with their armies, bringing with them their creed and carrying their Cross. They were able to defeat the Moslems for a while, but the Moslems were able to retrieve the land only when they stood under the wing of their religious banner, united their word, hallowed the name of Allah and surged out fighting under the leadership of Salah ed-Din al-Ayyubi. They fought for almost twenty years and at the end the Crusaders were defeated and Palestine was liberated.

"Say unto those who believe not, Ye shall be overcome, and thrown together into hell; an unhappy couch it shall be." (The Family of Imran—verse 12).

This is the only way to liberate Palestine. There is no doubt about the testimony of history. It is one of the laws of the universe and one of the rules of existence. Nothing can overcome iron except iron. Their false futile creed can only be defeated by the righteous Islamic creed. A creed could not be fought except by a creed, and in the last analysis, victory is for the just, for justice is certainly victorious.

"Our word hath formerly been given unto our servants the apostles; that they should certainly be assisted against the infidels, and that our armies should surely be the conquerors." (Those Who Rank Themselves—verses 171–172).

Article Thirty-Five:
The Islamic Resistance Movement views seriously the defeat of the Crusaders at the hands of Salah ed-Din al-Ayyubi and the rescuing of Palestine from their hands, as well as the defeat of the Tatars at Ein Galot, breaking their power at the hands of Qataz and Al-Dhaher Bivers and saving the Arab world from the Tatar onslaught which aimed at the destruction of every meaning of human civilization. The Movement draws lessons and examples from all this. The present Zionist onslaught has also been preceded by Crusading raids from the West and other Tatar raids from the East. Just as the Moslems faced those raids and planned fighting and defeating them, they should be able to confront the Zionist invasion and defeat it. This is indeed no problem for the Almighty Allah, provided that the intentions are pure, the determination is true and that Moslems have benefited from past experiences, rid themselves of the effects of ideological invasion and followed the customs of their ancestors.

The Islamic Resistance Movement is Composed of Soldiers: Article Thirty-Six:

While paving its way, the Islamic Resistance Movement, emphasizes time and again to all the sons of our people, to the Arab and Islamic nations, that it does not seek personal fame, material gain, or social prominence. It does not aim to compete against any one from among our people, or take his place. Nothing of the sort at all. It will not act against any of the sons of Moslems or those who are peaceful towards it from among non-Moslems, be they here or anywhere else. It will only serve as a support for all groupings and organizations operating against the Zionist enemy and its lackeys.

The Islamic Resistance Movement adopts Islam as its way of life. Islam is its creed and religion. Whoever takes Islam as his way of life, be it an organization, a grouping, a country or any other body, the Islamic Resistance Movement considers itself as their soldiers and nothing more.

We ask Allah to show us the right course, to make us an example to others and to judge between us and our people with truth. "O Lord, do thou judge between us and our nation with truth; for thou art the best judge." (Al Araf—Verse 89).

The last of our prayers will be praise to Allah, the Master of the Universe.

Hamas General Principles and Policies (2017)

In the Name of Allah Most Gracious Most Merciful
The Islamic Resistance Movement "Hamas"

A Document of General Principles and Policies

Praise be to Allah, the Lord of all worlds. May the peace and blessings of Allah be upon Muhammad, the Master of Messengers and the Leader of the mujahidin, and upon his household and all his companions.

Preamble:

Palestine is the land of the Arab Palestinian people, from it they originate, to it they adhere and belong, and about it they reach out and communicate.

Palestine is a land whose status has been elevated by Islam, a faith that holds it in high esteem, that breathes through it its spirit and just values and that lays the foundation for the doctrine of defending and protecting it.

Palestine is the cause of a people who have been let down by a world that fails to secure their rights and restore to them what has been usurped from them, a people whose land continues to suffer one of the worst types of occupation in this world.

Palestine is a land that was seized by a racist, anti-human and colonial Zionist project that was founded on a false promise (the Balfour Declaration), on recognition of a usurping entity and on imposing a fait accompli by force.

Palestine symbolizes the resistance that shall continue until liberation is accomplished, until the return is fulfilled and until a fully sovereign state is established with Jerusalem as its capital.

Palestine is the true partnership among Palestinians of all affiliations for the sublime objective of liberation.

Palestine is the spirit of the Ummah and its central cause; it is the soul of humanity and its living conscience.

This document is the product of deep deliberations that led us to a strong consensus. As a movement, we agree about both the theory and the practice of the vision that is outlined in the pages that follow. It is a vision that stands on solid grounds and on well-established principles. This document unveils the goals, the milestones and the way in which national unity can be enforced. It also establishes our common understanding of the Palestinian cause, the working principles which we use to further it, and the limits of flexibility used to interpret it.

The Movement:
1. The Islamic Resistance Movement "Hamas" is a Palestinian Islamic national liberation and resistance movement. Its goal is to liberate Palestine and confront the Zionist project. Its frame of reference is Islam, which determines its principles, objectives and means.

The Land of Palestine:
2. Palestine, which extends from the River Jordan in the east to the Mediterranean in the west and from Ras Al-Naqurah in the north to Umm Al-Rashrash in the south, is an integral territorial unit. It is the land and the home of the Palestinian people. The expulsion and banishment of the Palestinian people from their land and the establishment of the Zionist entity therein do not annul the right of the Palestinian people to their entire land and do not entrench any rights therein for the usurping Zionist entity.

3. Palestine is an Arab Islamic land. It is a blessed sacred land that has a special place in the heart of every Arab and every Muslim.

The Palestinian People:

4. The Palestinians are the Arabs who lived in Palestine until 1947, irrespective of whether they were expelled from it, or stayed in it; and every person that was born to an Arab Palestinian father after that date, whether inside or outside Palestine, is a Palestinian.

5. The Palestinian identity is authentic and timeless; it is passed from generation to generation. The catastrophes that have befallen the Palestinian people, as a consequence of the Zionist occupation and its policy of displacement, cannot erase the identity of the Palestinian people nor can they negate it. A Palestinian shall not lose his or her national identity or rights by acquiring a second nationality.

6. The Palestinian people are one people, made up of all Palestinians, inside and outside of Palestine, irrespective of their religion, culture or political affiliation.

Islam and Palestine:

7. Palestine is at the heart of the Arab and Islamic Ummah and enjoys a special status. Within Palestine there exists Jerusalem, whose precincts are blessed by Allah. Palestine is the Holy Land, which Allah has blessed for humanity. It is the Muslims' first Qiblah and the destination of the journey performed at night by Prophet Muhammad, peace be upon him. It is the location from where he ascended to the upper heavens. It is the birthplace of Jesus Christ, peace be upon him. Its soil contains the remains of thousands of Prophets, Companions and Mujahidin. It is the land of people who are determined to defend the truth—within Jerusalem and its surroundings—who are not deterred or intimidated by those who oppose them and by those who betray them, and they will continue their mission until the Promise of Allah is fulfilled.

8. By virtue of its justly balanced middle way and moderate spirit, Islam—for Hamas—provides a comprehensive way of life and an order that is fit for purpose at all times and in all places. Islam is a religion of peace and tolerance. It provides an umbrella for the followers of other creeds and religions who can practice their beliefs in security and safety. Hamas also believes that Palestine has always been and will always be a model of coexistence, tolerance and civilizational innovation.

9. Hamas believes that the message of Islam upholds the values of truth, justice, freedom and dignity and prohibits all forms of injustice and incriminates oppressors irrespective of their religion, race, gender or nationality. Islam is against all forms of religious, ethnic or sectarian extremism and bigotry. It is the religion that inculcates in its followers the value of standing up to aggression and of supporting the oppressed; it motivates them to give generously and make sacrifices in defence of their dignity, their land, their peoples and their holy places.

Jerusalem:

10. Jerusalem is the capital of Palestine. Its religious, historic and civilizational status is fundamental to the Arabs, Muslims and the world at large. Its Islamic and Christian holy places belong exclusively to the Palestinian people and to the Arab and Islamic Ummah. Not one stone of Jerusalem can be surrendered or relinquished. The measures undertaken by the occupiers in Jerusalem, such as Judaization, settlement building, and establishing facts on the ground are fundamentally null and void.

11. The blessed Al-Aqsa Mosque belongs exclusively to our people and our Ummah, and the occupation has no right to it whatsoever. The occupation's plots, measures and attempts to judaize Al-Aqsa and divide it are null, void and illegitimate.

The Refugees and the Right of Return:

12. The Palestinian cause in its essence is a cause of an occupied land and a displaced people. The right of the Palestinian refugees and the displaced to return to their homes from which they were banished or were banned from returning to—whether in the lands occupied in 1948 or in 1967 (that is the whole of Palestine), is a natural right, both individual and collective. This right is confirmed by all divine laws as well as by the basic principles of human rights and international law. It is an inalienable right and cannot be dispensed with by any party, whether Palestinian, Arab or international.

13. Hamas rejects all attempts to erase the rights of the refugees, including the attempts to settle them outside Palestine and through the projects of the alternative homeland. Compensation to the Palestinian refugees for the harm they have suffered as a consequence of banishing them and occupying their land is an absolute right that goes hand in hand with their right to return. They are to receive compensation upon their return and this does not negate or diminish their right to return.

The Zionist Project:

14. The Zionist project is a racist, aggressive, colonial and expansionist project based on seizing the properties of others; it is hostile to the Palestinian people and to their aspiration for freedom, liberation, return and self-determination. The Israeli entity is the plaything of the Zionist project and its base of aggression.

15. The Zionist project does not target the Palestinian people alone; it is the enemy of the Arab and Islamic Ummah posing a grave threat to its security and interests. It is also hostile to the Ummah's aspirations for unity, renaissance and liberation and has been the major source of its troubles. The Zionist project also poses a danger to international security and peace and to mankind and its interests and stability.

16. Hamas affirms that its conflict is with the Zionist project not with the Jews because of their religion. Hamas does not wage a struggle against the Jews because they are Jewish but wages a struggle against the Zionists who occupy Palestine. Yet, it is the Zionists who constantly identify Judaism and the Jews with their own colonial project and illegal entity.

17. Hamas rejects the persecution of any human being or the undermining of his or her rights on nationalist, religious or sectarian grounds. Hamas is of the view that the Jewish problem, anti-Semitism and the persecution of the Jews are phenomena fundamentally linked to European history and not to the history of the Arabs and the Muslims or to their heritage. The Zionist movement, which was able with the help of Western powers to occupy Palestine, is the most dangerous form of settlement occupation which has already disappeared from much of the world and must disappear from Palestine.

The Position toward Occupation and Political Solutions:

18. The following are considered null and void: the Balfour Declaration, the British Mandate Document, the UN Palestine Partition Resolution, and whatever resolutions and measures that derive from them or are similar to them. The establishment of "Israel" is entirely illegal and contravenes the inalienable rights of the Palestinian people and goes against their will and the will of the Ummah; it is also in violation of human rights that are guaranteed by international conventions, foremost among them is the right to self-determination.

19. There shall be no recognition of the legitimacy of the Zionist entity. Whatever has befallen the land of Palestine in terms of occupation, settlement building, Judaization or changes to its features or falsification of facts is illegitimate. Rights never lapse.

20. Hamas believes that no part of the land of Palestine shall be compromised or conceded, irrespective of the causes, the circumstances and the pressures and no matter how long the occupation lasts. Hamas rejects any alternative to the full and complete liberation of Palestine, from the river to the sea. However, without compromising its rejection of the Zionist entity and without relinquishing any Palestinian rights, Hamas considers the establishment of a fully sovereign and independent Palestinian state, with Jerusalem as its capital along the lines of the 4th of June 1967, with the return of the refugees and the displaced to their homes from which they were expelled, to be a formula of national consensus.

21. Hamas affirms that the Oslo Accords and their addenda contravene the governing rules of international law in that they generate commitments that violate the inalienable rights of the Palestinian people. Therefore, the Movement rejects these agreements and all that flows from them, such as the obligations that are detrimental to the interests of our people, especially security coordination (collaboration).

22. Hamas rejects all the agreements, initiatives and settlement projects that are aimed at undermining the Palestinian cause and the rights of our Palestinian people. In this regard, any stance, initiative or political programme must not in any way violate these rights and should not contravene them or contradict them.

23. Hamas stresses that transgression against the Palestinian people, usurping their land and banishing them from their homeland cannot be called peace. Any settlements reached on this basis will not lead to peace. Resistance and jihad for the liberation of Palestine will remain a legitimate right, a duty and an honour for all the sons and daughters of our people and our Ummah.

Resistance and Liberation:

24. The liberation of Palestine is the duty of the Palestinian people in particular and the duty of the Arab and Islamic Ummah in general. It is also a humanitarian obligation as necessitated by the dictates of truth and justice. The agencies working for Palestine, whether national, Arab, Islamic or humanitarian, complement each other and are harmonious and not in conflict with each other.

25. Resisting the occupation with all means and methods is a legitimate right guaranteed by divine laws and by international norms and laws. At the heart of these lies armed resistance, which is regarded as the strategic choice for protecting the principles and the rights of the Palestinian people.

26. Hamas rejects any attempt to undermine the resistance and its arms. It also affirms the right of our people to develop the means and mechanisms of resistance. Managing resistance, in terms of escalation or de-escalation, or in terms of diversifying the means and methods, is an integral part of the process of managing the conflict and should not be at the expense of the principle of resistance.

The Palestinian Political System:

27. A real state of Palestine is a state that has been liberated. There is no alternative to a fully sovereign Palestinian State on the entire national Palestinian soil, with Jerusalem as its capital.

28. Hamas believes in, and adheres to, managing its Palestinian relations on the basis of pluralism, democracy, national partnership, acceptance of the other and the adoption of dialogue. The aim is to bolster the unity of ranks and joint action for the purpose of accomplishing national goals and fulfilling the aspirations of the Palestinian people.

29. The PLO is a national framework for the Palestinian people inside and outside of Palestine. It should therefore be preserved, developed and rebuilt on democratic foundations so as to secure the participation of all the constituents and forces of the Palestinian people, in a manner that safeguards Palestinian rights.

30. Hamas stresses the necessity of building Palestinian national institutions on sound democratic principles, foremost among them are free and fair elections. Such process should be on the basis of national partnership and in accordance with a clear programme and a clear strategy that adhere to the rights, including the right of resistance, and which fulfil the aspirations of the Palestinian people.

31. Hamas affirms that the role of the Palestinian Authority should be to serve the Palestinian people and safeguard their security, their rights and their national project.

32. Hamas stresses the necessity of maintaining the independence of Palestinian national decision-making. Outside forces should not be allowed to intervene. At the same time, Hamas affirms the responsibility of the Arabs and the Muslims and their duty and role in the liberation of Palestine from Zionist occupation.

33. Palestinian society is enriched by its prominent personalities, figures, dignitaries, civil society institutions, and youth, students, trade unionist and women's groups who together work for the achievement of national goals and societal building, pursue resistance, and achieve liberation.

34. The role of Palestinian women is fundamental in the process of building the present and the future, just as it has always been in the process of making Palestinian history. It is a pivotal role in the project of resistance, liberation and building the political system.

The Arab and Islamic Ummah:

35. Hamas believes that the Palestinian issue is the central cause for the Arab and Islamic Ummah.

36. Hamas believes in the unity of the Ummah with all its diverse constituents and is aware of the need to avoid anything that could fragment the Ummah and undermine its unity.

37. Hamas believes in cooperating with all states that support the rights of the Palestinian people. It opposes intervention in the internal affairs of any country. It also refuses to be drawn into disputes and conflicts that take place among different countries. Hamas adopts the policy of opening up to different states in the world, especially the Arab and Islamic states. It endeavours to establish balanced relations on the basis of combining the requirements of the Palestinian cause and the Palestinian people's interests on the one hand with the interests of the Ummah, its renaissance and its security on the other.

The Humanitarian and International Aspect:

38. The Palestinian issue is one that has major humanitarian and international dimensions. Supporting and backing this cause is a humanitarian and civilizational task that is required by the prerequisites of truth, justice and common humanitarian values.

39. From a legal and humanitarian perspective, the liberation of Palestine is a legitimate activity, it is an act of self-defence, and it is the expression of the natural right of all peoples to self-determination.

40. In its relations with world nations and peoples, Hamas believes in the values of cooperation, justice, freedom and respect of the will of the people.

41. Hamas welcomes the stances of states, organisations and institutions that support the rights of the Palestinian people. It salutes the free peoples of the world who support the Palestinian cause. At the same time, it denounces the support granted by any party to the Zionist entity or the attempts to cover up its crimes and aggression against the Palestinians and calls for the prosecution of Zionist war criminals.

42. Hamas rejects the attempts to impose hegemony on the Arab and Islamic Ummah just as it rejects the attempts to impose hegemony on the rest of the world's nations and peoples. Hamas also condemns all forms of colonialism, occupation, discrimination, oppression and aggression in the world.

National Lawyers Guild International Committee Statement

NLG International emphasizes Palestinian right to resist, stands in solidarity with Palestine

The National Lawyers Guild emphasizes the legitimacy of the right of the Palestinian people to resist illegal military occupation, apartheid, and ethnic cleansing, and urges the United States to stop enabling and arming Israel's perpetration of its atrocities. The NLG stands in solidarity with the people of Palestine in their struggle against the settler colonial state of Israel and calls on our members and allies throughout the United States and around the globe to stand and act in support of that struggle.

The United States government not only immediately condemned the recent military actions carried out by Palestinian resistance after it has spent decades supporting and enabling Israeli atrocities against the Palestinian people that are the direct cause of the current actions; in fact, U.S. President Joe Biden announced a commitment to "emergency aid" in the form of additional weaponry to be sent to the Israeli occupation regime. This comes atop the existing nearly $4 billion in U.S. military aid to Israel every year. These condemnations have been echoed by politicians across the U.S. political spectrum, including those who campaign as progressives and anti-racists.

The National Lawyers Guild urges public recognition of the right to resist unlawful occupation "by all available means, including armed struggle," as noted in United Nations General Assembly Res. 37/43. Armed struggle "against colonial domination and alien occupation and against racist regimes in the exercise of their right of self-determination" is explicitly contemplated under the Geneva Conventions. Major human rights organizations have recognized through detailed investigation and findings that Israel is perpetrating apartheid, a crime against humanity, against the Palestinian people.[1]

Instead of condemning Palestinian resistance, the U.S. is obliged under international law to cut off all military, financial and political support that enables Israel's brutal occupation. The U.S. ruling elite has shown its blatant hypocrisy and morally unfathomable racist and imperialist agenda by unconditionally and continuously supporting Israeli violence and oppression against Palestinians on a permanent basis, and then expressing outrage at any Palestinian resistance.

By continuing the flow of weapons and aid to Israel, the United States is participating as an aider and abetter of apartheid and attempted genocide in Palestine, for which U.S. officials can and must be held accountable. The United States continues to designate Palestinian resistance organizations as "Foreign Terrorist Organizations," despite the fact that they are engaged in exercising their fundamental and protected right to self-defense and to liberate their land and people from occupation and colonialism. These lists allow for the persecution, criminalization and economic coercion of people resisting apartheid, genocide and colonialism, which is itself a crime. We call for all Palestinian and Lebanese resistance

---

1　Human Rights Watch, "A Threshold Crossed: Israeli Authorities and the Crimes of Apartheid and Persecution," April 27, 2021. https://www.hrw.org /report/2021/04/27/threshold-crossed/israeli-authorities-and-crimes-apartheid-and-persecution; Amnesty International, "Israel's Apartheid Against Palestinians: Cruel System of Domination and Crime Against Humanity," 2022, https://www .amnesty.org/en/documents/mde15/5141/2022/en/; Btselem, "A regime of Jewish Supremacy from the Jordan River to the Mediterranean Sea: This is Apartheid," 12 January 2021, https://www.btselem.org/publications/fulltext/202101_this_is_ apartheid; Al-Haq, "Israeli Apartheid: Tool of Zionist Settler Colonialism," 29 Nov. 2022, https://www.alhaq.org/advocacy/20931.html.

organizations to be removed from the U.S. list of "Foreign Terrorist Organizations" and "Specially Designated Global Terrorists."

Palestinians have repeatedly called for boycott, divestment and sanctions against Israel, a call adopted 16 years ago by the NLG. We reiterate our statement of May 2021, "Statement in Solidarity with the People of Palestine in their Struggle Against the Settler Colonial State of Israel," in which we noted: "Arab states have imposed a boycott of Israel for decades for its ongoing occupation of Arab land, including Palestinian and Syrian land. The United States has expended a tremendous amount of military and financial pressure to undermine and break the Arab boycott of Israel, from the Camp David accords with Egypt in 1978 to the more recent attempts at a "deal of the century" and the "Abraham Accords." These normalization campaigns, sponsored and funded by the United States, aim to expand the complicity of Arab states with Israeli war crimes and crimes against humanity while denying the Palestinian people international support. Normalization with Israel is a U.S. project designed to advance Israeli impunity."

At this historic moment, we reiterate our calls and commitments of two years ago. As a community of legal workers and advocates who prioritize human rights and support for justice and liberation of oppressed people, we must stand firm in our solidarity by:

- **Clearly and unequivocally condemning Israeli state** and colonial violence against the Palestinian people from Gaza to Jerusalem, in the West Bank and throughout historical Palestine.
- **Escalating our pursuit for legal accountability for Israeli colonial violence,** ethnic cleansing, ongoing war crimes and crimes against humanity, including the crime of apartheid, in our global and local legal institutions.
- **Affirming the legal right of all Palestinian refugees to return to Palestine.** International law upholds the Palestinian right to return. U.N. General Assembly Resolution 3236 (1974) reaffirms the inalienable rights of the Palestinian people to self-determination, national independence and sovereignty,

and the right of Palestinians to return to their homes and property.

- **Affirming and protecting the legal right of Palestinians to resist the colonizing power that seeks to annihilate them.** International law also upholds the right of self-defense for peoples under colonial and foreign domination and subjugation, "reaffirm[ing] the legitimacy of the struggle of peoples for independence, territorial integrity, national unity and liberation from colonial and foreign domination and foreign occupation by all available means, including armed struggle."

- **Demanding the release of all Palestinian prisoners** and an end the use of torture and administrative detention. There are currently approximately 5,250 Palestinian prisoners in Israeli jails, including nearly 1,350 jailed without charge or trial under arbitrary and unlawful administrative detention, as well as 39 women and 170 children.

- **Supporting the call for boycott, divestment and sanctions** of all institutions whose conduct is complicit in Israeli crimes, complicit in Israeli apartheid, complicit in the occupation of Palestine, or complicit in any denial of Palestinian human rights.

- **Defending the Palestinian movement and community in the United States,** including students, activists, and scholars who are targeted by Zionist lawfare institutions for their support of Palestinian human rights, and the criminalization, surveillance and harassment of Palestinians by U.S. political and police forces.

- **Demanding an end to U.S. aid to Israel and holding all U.S. leaders accountable for their political support for Israel's crimes.** Israel is committing these human rights violations with U.S. aid, in violation of the U.S. Arms Export Control and Foreign Assistance acts.

- **Demanding that the United States stop its political and economic intimidation, including sanctions,** to pressure states to normalize relations with Israel.

The National Lawyers Guild was formed in 1937 as the first national, racially integrated bar association in the U.S. to advocate for the protection of constitutional, human, and civil rights.

Statement by the National Lawyers Guild International Committee[2]

October 8, 2023

---

2   "NLG International Emphasizes Palestinian Right to Resist, Stands in Solidarity with Palestine," National Lawyers Guild International Committee, October 8, 2023, https://nlginternational.org/2023/10/nlg-international-emphasizes-palestinian-right-to-resist-stands-in-solidarity-with-palestine/.

Muslim Anti-Zionist Reads Dershowitz's Book and Becomes a Zionist[1]

I was born to hate Jews. It was part of my life. I never questioned it. I was not born in Iran or Syria. I was born in England. My parents moved there from Pakistan. Theirs was the typical immigrant story; moved to the West in the hope of making a better life for themselves and their children. We were a devout Muslim family but not extremist or radical in any way.

We only wish the best for everyone. Everyone except the Jews. The Jews we believed were aliens living on stolen Muslim land. Occupiers who were engaged in a genocide against the Palestinian people. Our hatred, therefore, was justified and righteous and it made me and my friends vulnerable to the arguments of radical extremists. If the Jews were as evil as we had always believed, mustn't those who support them, Christians, Americans, and others in the West be just as evil?

Beginning in the 1990s speakers and teachers of mosques and in schools began to endlessly repeat this theme. We were not Western, we were not British, we were Muslims first and only. Our loyalty was

---

1   Kasim Hafeez, "Born to Hate Jews," Prager U, December 5, 2016, https://www .prageru.com/video/born-to-hate-jews.

to our religion and to our fellow Muslims. We owe nothing to the Western nations that welcomed us as Westerners. They were our enemies. All of this had its desired effect, at least it did on me. It changed the way that I saw the world. I began to see the suffering of Muslims including in Britain as the fault of Western imperialism. The West was at war with us, and the Jews controlled the West.

My experience at university in Britain only enhanced my increasingly radical beliefs. Hating Israel was a badge of honor. Stage an anti-Israel pro-Palestinian rally and you're sure to draw a large approving crowd. While at university, I decided the protests and propaganda against Israel were not enough. True jihad demanded violence, so I made plans to join the real fight. I would leave college and join a terrorist training camp in Pakistan, but fortunately for me, fate intervened in a bookstore.

I came across a book called *The Case for Israel* by Harvard Law professor Alan Dershowitz. The case for Israel? What case could there be? The title itself made me furious and I began to read the pages almost as an act of defiance. How ill-informed, how stupid could this guy be to defend the indefensible. Well, he was a Jew. That had to be the answer. Still, I read, and what I read challenged all of my dogmas about Israel and the Jews. I read that it wasn't Israel that created the Palestinian refugee crisis, it was the Arab countries, the United Nations, and the corrupt Palestinian leadership. I read that Jews didn't exploit the Holocaust to create the state of Israel. The movement to create a modern Jewish state dated back to the nineteenth century and ultimately to the beginnings of the Jewish people almost four thousand years ago, and I read that Israel is not engaged in genocide against the Palestinians. On the contrary, the Palestinian population has actually doubled in just twenty years.

All this did was make me angrier. I needed to prove this was wrong, to see with my own eyes how racist and oppressive Israel really was. So I bought a plane ticket. I will travel to Israel, the home of my enemy and that's when everything changed. Everything. What I saw with my own eyes was even more challenging than what Dershowitz had written. Instead of apartheid, I saw Muslims, Christians, and Jews coexisting. Instead of hate, I saw acceptance and even compassion. I saw a raucous modern liberal democracy, full of flaws certainly. The fundamentally decent. I saw a country that wanted nothing more than to live in peace with its neighbors. I saw my hatred melting before my eyes.

I knew right then what I had to do. Too many people on this planet consumed with the same hatred that consumed me. They have been taught to despise the Jewish state. Many Muslims by their religion, many others by their college professors or student groups. So here is my challenge to anyone who feels this way: do what I did. Seek out the truth for yourself. If the truth could change me, it can change anyone. I'm Kasim Hafeez for Prager University.

A Conversation with Elon Musk about Censorship and Anti-Semitism[1]

Alan Dershowitz: I have been studying the issue of free speech for seventy years and let me start with a statement that many will disagree with. No country in history has ever really tested free speech, has ever seen whether the marketplace of ideas works—whether we can really have a society without censorship, a society where every idea is tested on their merits. This cannot be a right-left issue. The issue has to be one of trying to live with complete and total free speech and because you may be the first person who has really tried. Thomas Jefferson didn't try, Alexander Hamilton didn't try, Abraham Lincoln didn't try. They all compromised. You were trying for the first time an experiment, a great experiment to see whether we can survive with the marketplace of ideas and without censorship.

I want to state unequivocally we should not be drawing lines. That's a mistake, to draw a line. That's an image that I want you to reject.

Musk: Okay.

---

1 Some editorial changes were made for clarity.

Dershowitz: We should draw instead a circle. I call it the circle of symmetry: that is, to create a situation where all thoughts and all ideas are treated equally. That we don't make judgments on the basis of whether something is anti-Semitic or pro-Semitic, pro-Jewish, anti-Jewish, pro-Christian, anti-Jew, pro-right, anti-right. We create a circle, a symmetrical circle in which things that are outside the circle, things that are illegal, such as abusing children, but anything else has to be within a circle, so if it's permitted for one "ism" it has to be permitted for the others. That's exactly what universities are failing to do. They're creating a line on which favored groups fall on one side and disfavored groups fall on the other side, and Elon, this is an incredible challenge to you.

Musk: Yeah.

Dershowitz: You should try to create a circle of symmetry. Can you try to figure out what are the parameters for what kind of speech can be censored, what kind of speech must be permitted, without focusing on the content of the speech itself—without focusing on whether it's right-left or anything of that kind? It has to be something that's absolutely neutral. Then I think you'll find very few people will want to censor because they'll realize that they can't have free speech for me but not for thee. Every time they try to censor their enemy, they will be censoring themselves, if we have a circle of ism symmetry rather than lines which are easily manipulable.

No idea should be censored. Oliver Wendell Holmes put it very well when he said every idea is an incitement. We can't draw lines between advocacy and incitement. We failed every time we've tried to do that, and so my suggestion to you is don't listen to the critics. Don't listen to the people who want to draw lines that are self-serving, that serve the Jewish community, that serve Israel. I don't want to draw those kinds of lines. I'm in favor of no prior censorship except things that are overtly illegal. Let the marketplace decide and make sure that there is an opportunity for everybody to answer. You can't draw a line on hate speech. One person's hate speech is another person's love speech. You have to open up the marketplace of ideas. That circle of ism symmetry will be self-enforcing. Nobody's going to censor the enemy when they know that they're going to be censoring themselves as well.

Musk: Yeah, and I should say, like, we are experimenting with this idea of freedom of speech but not reach. Meaning you could, you can post anything on the platform even if it is hateful provided it is lawful. But there's a separate question of then is that promoted or not promoted. You know, does that enter our recommendation engine, and if so, with what promise. And you know our current approach is to say, okay, you can say things that are hateful but legal on the platform, but we are not going to recommend that to others. That's the current approach that we have.

Dershowitz: You can see how that can be abused and become a form of censorship too.

Musk: I know. I agree. It's advertisers, certainly, [who] have a right to say what content they will appear next to because that's their right too, but not to dictate what can be said on the platform.

Dershowitz: I agree with that. I think there's one other danger, and the danger is reflected by the people who have been selected to join this conversation. I think there is a danger of this being perceived as a right-wing reaction to left-wing censorship. I myself am somebody who's liberal. I identify more with the left than the right, but I strongly oppose efforts by the left as well as by the right to censor. It would be a very serious mistake if X or you were perceived as some way implicitly favoring the right over the left. I would suggest that you have a small group of people, who represent different perspectives. I would represent left perspective to make sure that you don't drift over to the right. Today the greatest danger to free speech comes from the left. Let's be clear about that.

Musk: Yeah, I agree.

Dershowitz: Violence comes from the right, they shoot synagogues. The left is educating our future leaders. I know, I taught at Harvard for fifty years. I know who our students are. They are the future presidents of the United States. So, the left poses a far greater danger of censoring free speech and of skewing the marketplace of ideas. X has to be perceived in reality as perfectly symmetrical.

Musk: That is our aspiration, that's our goal. Now the reality of it for anyone who's paying attention, and I'm sure you saw this prior to the acquisition, Twitter was very left and getting even more left. They had a massive thumb on the scale on elections. Frankly, worldwide on the side of the left and would suppress press, you know, Republican voices at a rate, I don't know, sometimes perhaps an order of magnitude greater than Democrats. So, there was a tremendous amount of bias. Now in moving and then coming from a system where it's like, okay there's a massive electoring [sic] bias to a system that is more inclusive and that could—where at least say 80 percent of America, perhaps the world—be on the platform and feel that it's a level playing field. And it's fair to people with a wide range of views. That's our goal and that's what we're doing now. Given that it started so far off the left, it is accurate to say it's moving right because it's moving to the center. So, it's technically true that it's moving right. Not that it suddenly popped over and instantaneously became, you know, from a left-wing propaganda arm to a right-wing propaganda arm, but necessarily if it was pretty damn far on the left it's going to have to move to the right in order to get to the center and that is that is our goal.

Dershowitz: With all due respect, I disagree with that. I don't think you move to the right in order to overcome the left. You move to the center directly and you create—

Musk: We are moving to the center directly. I'm just saying, you know, as Einstein would say all motion is relative. If you start on the left, and you move to the center, you're necessarily moving right. That's what I'm saying. Our goal is not to move to the right, it is that we are moving right in order to get to the center. That's, you know, it has to be.

Dershowitz: I would put it differently. I would say you're moving away from the left to the center.

Musk: Correct, which is perceived by the left as moving right.

Dershowitz: But if you look at the people who are on this call. I think it is fair for some people to perceive this as a movement to the right. You don't want to be perceived that way. You have to make it absolutely clear that you are the only platform in the world that doesn't take a left-right position—pro-Jewish or anti-Jewish, pro-Christian, pro-American. That you are a platform that is pro-free speech. You're the first people in history ever to try to create a true marketplace of ideas. John Stuart Mill advocated it, Jefferson advocated it. Nobody has ever achieved it. You're in a position where you can achieve it, but don't destroy it by being perceived as a right-wing reaction to left-wing excesses. You must be perceived as being from the center, and everything you do is designed to create a neutral space—a marketplace of ideas where the only answer to false speech is true speech and where the marketplace determines how much the speech is spread out, how many people listen to it.

Musk: Yeah.

Dershowitz: We have to have more confidence in our ability to answer bad speech. I accept that challenge in my life, and I don't want to censor my enemies.

Musk: Yeah, absolutely. And to be clear, we actually have massively broadened what can be said on the platform. But we have, and perhaps you disagree with this, but we have tried to guide our algorithm to promote things that are positive more than things that are negative to frankly to have a love bias if you will. No, I realize that's perhaps, this is not in terms of what can be said, but in terms of what is promoted to others. And you know, if somebody wants to say, like you know, accuse me of saying, well it's wrong to have a slight, maybe you know, a bias towards love and positivity, then I'm rightly accused of that.

Dershowitz: Look, I agree, this is a long conversation. I think we can contribute to helping make this into the first true, true marketplace of ideas.

Musk: Well, thank you. I think our overlap in agreement is very high, so I would certainly value your opinion in the future because this is something that we should debate frequently, and like I said, I think the overarching goal is how to make this platform serve as a positive force for humanity. And I think the free exchange of ideas does result in a positive force for humanity, and if somebody feels like their ideas are, even if they're wrong, that they're not being sort of squashed and censored, then I think, because I think being squashed and censored breeds that hatred and resentment and simply also then sends people to perhaps hate echo chambers that are outside of the mainstream. I think where you get some of the sort of, you know, people who go kill, mass shooting, because they're in some sort of hate echo chamber.

Dershowitz: I agree, and I think you're the only one out there who can do that now, and I think we all should sacrifice our own interests, even on issues like anti-Semitism, to a far greater humanitarian interest in promoting open and complete dialogue. Complete free speech in the marketplace of ideas. Only you can do that.

Musk: Well, thank you. I'll do my best here and your sort of advice would certainly be very much appreciated. You know, I believe one is always wrong to some degree, and we simply aspire to be a little less wrong over time, and eventually we can, you know, have to get to a really good place. So, like I said, the idea is how do we make this a positive force for humanity, where we increase the sum of human knowledge. It's a place where people, you know, if their ideas are based on false premises, especially hateful ideas that we can perhaps point out that the reason that they have this hatred is because of things that aren't true. It's like actually you're hating this or that group for things that are not true, or perhaps in some cases, things that happened a long time ago for which people no longer_You know, it's like it was a great-great-grandfather or something, that did the bad thing. So that's why I say like I think there's a lot of wisdom in forgiveness and turning the other cheek, and when I was younger, I actually thought, well, turn the other cheek, isn't that a sign of weakness? But I think it is actually a sign of strength. Now, by the same token, if you turn the other cheek and you're just getting slapped all day, at a certain point, you stop turning the cheek. But the general notion of forgiveness is incredibly important. Don't hold some grudge for a long time, in some cases centuries. It's like, let it go, and you know, take a quote from the New Testament that, "The truth shall set you free," as John said. Truth shall set you free. I'm a big believer that the road to morality is, in my view, truth and curiosity. And if you care about truth, and you're curious, I think that is a natural outflowing from that.

Letter to the President of Harvard University by William A. Ackman

November 4, 2023

Dear President Gay,

I am writing this letter to you regretfully. Never did I think I would have to write a letter to the president of my alma mater about the impact of her actions and inactions on the health and safety of its student body in order to help catalyze necessary change. For the past four weeks since the horrors of October 7th, I have been in dialogue with members of the corporation board, other alumni, as well as students and faculty sharing and comparing our concerns about the growing number of antisemitic incidents on campus, as we wait for you and the University to act. Four weeks after the barbaric terrorist acts of October 7th, I have lost confidence that you and the University will do what is required.

Last Wednesday, I spent seven hours on campus meeting with Jewish, Israeli, and non-Jewish students and faculty at the Law School, at HBS and in a 90-minute town hall in Aldrich 112 with 230 Jewish college students (coincidentally, one for each hostage held by Hamas), research staff, and faculty from the University at large, organized by Harvard Chabad. Over the course of the day, it became clear that the situation at Harvard is dire and getting worse, much worse than I had realized.

Jewish students are being bullied, physically intimidated, spat on, and in several widely disseminated videos of one such incident, physically assaulted. Student Slack message boards are replete with antisemitic statements, memes, and images. On-campus protesters on the Widener Library steps and elsewhere shout "Intifada! Intifada! Intifada! From the River to the Sea, Palestine Shall Be Free!" as they knowingly call for violent insurrection and use eliminationist language seeking the destruction of the State of Israel and the Jewish people.

When you explained in your October 12th video address that Harvard "embraces a commitment to free expression," you sent a clear message that the eliminationist and antisemitic statements of the protesters are permissible on campus. Putting aside the legal limitations on free speech that include restrictions on fighting words and true threats, "where speakers direct a threat to a person or group of persons with the intent of placing the victim in fear of bodily harm or death," if Harvard indeed had a strong track record of protecting free speech, many would have taken your support for free speech more seriously. Unfortunately, Harvard has not embraced a serious commitment to free speech, particularly so in recent years.

In The Foundation for Individual Rights and Expression (FIRE) Annual College Free Speech Rankings, Harvard has consistently finished in the bottom quartile in each of the past four years, with its ranking deteriorating each year. On September 23rd, just two weeks prior to October 7th, FIRE announced that Harvard achieved its lowest free speech ranking ever for the 2023 academic year, ranking last out of 254 universities, with a rating of 0.00, the only university with an "abysmal" speech climate. See: thefire.org/news/harvard-g… the results of the survey where FIRE cites multiple examples of incidents on the Harvard campus where students and faculty were denied their First Amendment rights. Therefore, when you cite Harvard's "commitment to free expression," in supporting the protesters, it rings false and hypocritical to the university at large and the Jewish community in particular.

Many Jewish students have also recently become afraid to express their concerns. Many have also felt the need to remove their mezuzahs, yarmulkes, Stars of David, and other overt evidence of their religion and heritage on campus and in Cambridge to avoid being exposed to discrimination, bullying or worse.

I am incredibly saddened to say that Harvard has also become a place where Jewish students are concerned about the threat of physical violence (which likely has a corresponding impact on their mental health) while among other insults, they are forced to sit next to classmates who openly and comfortably post, under their actual names, antisemitic statements and imagery on the student-wide Slack message system with no consequences for their actions.

And it is not just the Jewish students and faculty that are up in arms. While on campus, I heard a constant refrain from non-Jewish members of the Harvard community:

Why are Claudine and the administration doing nothing about this?

Harvard's Office of Equity, Diversity, Inclusion and Belonging

I have heard from many members of the Harvard community that Harvard's Office of Equity, Diversity, Inclusion and Belonging ("OEDIB") is an important contributing factor to the problem. I was surprised to learn from students and faculty that the OEDIB does not support Jewish, Asian and non-LGBTQIA White students. I had never read the OEDIB DEI statement until today when I wrote this letter. The DEI statement makes clear that Harvard's conception of diversity, equity, inclusion and belonging does not include Jews (at least those that are not in one of the other welcomed DEI groups). According to Harvard's DEI statement:

"We actively seek and welcome people of color, women, persons with disabilities, people who identify as LGBTQIA, and those who are at the intersections of these identities, from across the spectrum of disciplines and methods to join us."

In other words, Jews and others who are not on the above list are not welcome to join. When antisemitism is widely prevalent on campus, and the DEI office – which "views diversity, equity, inclusion and belonging as the pathway to achieving inclusive excellence and fostering a campus culture where everyone can thrive" – does not welcome Jewish students, we have a serious problem. It is abundantly clear that the campus culture that is being fostered at Harvard today is not one where everyone is included, feels a sense of belonging, welcomes diversity, or is a place where "everyone can thrive."

Equity on Campus

The issue of equity, or the lack thereof, was another issue about which I heard constant complaints, i.e., the so-called "double standard." One member of the faculty rhetorically asked:

"What would Claudine do if 34 Harvard student organizations put out a statement on May 25th, 2020 that 'George Floyd had it coming,'" noting that you have yet to condemn the student organization letter which holds Israel "solely responsible" for the heinous and barbaric acts of a terrorist organization.

Other faculty, alumni and students asked other rhetorical questions including:

"How would Harvard respond if a trans student attempted to walk by an anti-LGBTQIA demonstration on the HBS campus and was subject to the same abuse that the Jewish HBS student experienced at the Free Palestine demonstration on October 18th?"

"How would you respond to a Harvard white supremacist protest where students shouted 'Tulsa! Tulsa! Tulsa! From the Atlantic to the Pacific, America should be free of Black people.'"

Would Harvard even permit the above demonstrations to take place on campus?

Despite the outburst of antisemitic activities and protests on campus, the first initiative that Harvard took to protect students was the establishment on October 24th of a task force to "support students experiencing doxxing, harassment, and online security issues following backlash against students allegedly affiliated with a statement that held Israel 'entirely responsible' for violence in the

Israel-Hamas conflict." The creation of this task force sent a very strong message that the University was not just ignoring the antisemitic incidents and threats to Jewish student safety on campus, but rather it was taking sides in the conflict by only supporting students who held Israel responsible for Hamas' vile acts.

In summary, your failure to condemn the barbaric acts of October 7th opened the door for a wave of anti-Israel attacks on campus that have led to a growing number of antisemitic protests and actions. Your subsequent two statements about October 7th to the University attempting to address the failings of your first letter were not taken seriously as many perceived those statements as being driven by pressure from the alumni community rather than reflecting a sincere and authentic understanding of the issues, and real empathy for Israel and the Jewish community.

The failure of your communications to the public and the University coupled with the fact that the first tangible action by the University was to protect those who blamed Israel has created a belief among the Jewish and Israeli community at Harvard that they are not deemed welcome nor worthy of protection by the University.

"Narrow Casting"

Finally, your announcement on Friday October 27th about launching a task force to address antisemitism and your statement that "Antisemitism has no place at Harvard" was welcomed by members of the Jewish community in attendance, but students who participated in my Thursday town hall were either unaware of that announcement or alternatively questioned your commitment to address antisemitism.

At my town hall, it was noted that your antisemitism speech was made only to Jewish students and parents at a Hillel Shabbat dinner, and a transcript of your remarks was only given to and published in the Foreword, a niche Jewish publication with a tiny subscriber base. Two members of the Harvard faculty described this as "narrow casting" to an affinity group rather than you making a serious public commitment to address antisemitism. One research fellow stated, and many in the room agreed, that they would only believe that you were committed to stamp out antisemitism at Harvard if you stood up in front of the entire Harvard community and made that commitment, and you then implemented tangible and decisive actions consistent with that commitment.

While the members of the Jewish community I met with at Harvard were happy to hear from an alum who was willing to listen, many students questioned why you have not sat down with students so that you can hear their concerns first-hand.

Antisemitism at Harvard Prior to October 7th

In the transcript of your speech published in the Forward, you said about antisemitism at Harvard: "For years, this university has done too little to confront its continuing presence. No longer."

Your remarks imply that antisemitism has been a serious issue at Harvard that has gone unaddressed for years. I have been an active alum for 35 years having attended the college and HBS, taught numerous classes on campus each year, have participated in many fireside chats with large student audiences, mentor current students and recent graduates on a regular basis, and have been a member of the Dean's Advisory Board at the business school for many years. During this period, I have neither experienced nor have I become aware of any antisemitic incidents at Harvard until beginning four weeks ago.

When I asked my daughter today about her experience with antisemitism at Harvard (she graduated in 2020), she described antisemitism when she was at Harvard as "non-existent." While I am sure it is possible if not likely that there have been some antisemitic incidents at Harvard over the last 35 years, the reality is that Harvard has been an extremely comfortable place to be Jewish and/or Israeli, up until the last four weeks.

In truth, the outburst at antisemitism at Harvard is a recent one and is largely due to your actions and inactions and that of the administration and the University at large in failing to appropriately address blatant antisemitism on campus.

How Can You Solve the Problem?

What I find particularly upsetting about recent events on campus is that the problem is not so difficult to address. I do not believe that antisemitism is widespread among the student body and faculty at Harvard. Rather, I believe that a small minority of students, faculty, and staff are antisemitic and the administration's inaction in confronting the problem head on have emboldened this antisemitic subset of the community to escalate their antisemitic actions because there have been no consequences for doing so.

Actions speak much louder than words. Members of the Harvard community have heard some words, but experienced no actions of substance to address antisemitism on campus. I would therefore recommend the following steps which I believe will dramatically reduce if not eliminate antisemitic acts at Harvard immediately.

First, the students involved in harassing and allegedly physically assaulting the HBS student on October 18th should be immediately suspended. I understand that the University is waiting for the outcome of a police department review of the situation to take action, but this makes no sense. It is clear from the multiple videos available of the incident that the conduct of the protesters involved does not meet the standards for student conduct outlined in the Harvard College Student Handbook, in particular Harvard's anti-bullying policies outlined in the Report & Recommendation from the Anti-Bullying Working Group adopted on September 1, 2023. ...mmunitymisconductpolicies.harvard.edu/reports-and-dr... These standards alone are enough to invoke Disciplinary Probation until such time as the police department investigation is completed. Harvard student disciplinary actions should not be outsourced to the police department.

Taking decisive action now will put all Harvard students, faculty and staff on notice that the University takes violations of Harvard's code of conduct seriously, and will bring great comfort to the Jewish community at Harvard that appropriate actions to reduce threats to their safety are being implemented.

Second, the protesters who have been chanting Intifada and other eliminationist statements should be subject to disciplinary action. There are multiple videos available of the various protests that would enable the University to identify the individuals involved who can then be referred to the Administrative Board where appropriate disciplinary action can be determined and acted upon.

Third, the University should review the student Slack message boards to identify those students who have made antisemitic statements or shared antisemitic imagery. These students should also be referred to the Administration Board for appropriate disciplinary action.

Fourth, the University should publicly reach out to students in an effort to obtain other examples of antisemitic acts that should also be carefully investigated, and for which appropriate disciplinary steps should be taken.

Because Harvard students are notoriously focused on their job and career prospects post-graduation, disciplinary actions by the administration for failure to meet the University's standards for appropriate conduct that become part of a student's permanent record should serve as an effective deterrent to overt antisemitic acts on campus. No law firm, corporation or graduate program will hire or admit an antisemitic or racist student. I note that the recent letter to the deans of law schools around the country signed by many of the top law firms in the U.S. has, I am told, already begun to have an effect in reducing antisemitic acts at the Law School.

Fifth, the University should form a task force to review the appropriateness of the activities of the OEDIB and whether its practice of excluding certain minority communities on campus, including Asian and Jewish students, is appropriate, which in fact may be contributing to discrimination against these groups on campus.

Sixth, the results of the antisemitism task force should be made public as promptly as possible so that we can better understand the sources of antisemitism at Harvard. Harvard's admissions practices should be reassessed to ascertain why the university is admitting racist students, and should consider revisions to the application process to enable the University to better screen the character of candidates for admission.

Seventh, as Harvard president, you should make clear that Harvard supports free speech on campus, but that certain kinds of hate speech as well as fighting words and incitement to violence are not consistent with Harvard's values or considered appropriate conduct for members of the Harvard community. In connection with your commitment to free speech, Harvard should form a task force to understand the constraints on free speech at Harvard that have led to it ranking last on FIRE's annual college survey, so the issues that have led to Harvard's last-place ranking can be addressed.

Violations of Title VI of the Civil Rights Act of 1964

On September 28, 2023, the Biden Administration issued a clarifying release stating that Title VI of the Civil Rights Act of 1964 prohibits certain forms of antisemitism, Islamophobia and related discrimination as part of its National Strategy to Counter Antisemitism released in May 2023 whitehouse.gov/wp-content/upl... Title VI of the Civil Rights Act requires universities to provide all students, including students who are or are perceived to be Jewish, a school environment free from discrimination. The consequences for a university's failure to meet the requirements of Title VI include the cancellation of federal funding.

Harvard has failed in recent weeks to meet its Title VI obligations which threatens a major source of the University's funding. When coupled with numerous Jewish and non-Jewish alumni that have publicly and privately shared these same concerns, important sources of Harvard's revenues are at risk. While the University should not need a financial incentive to eliminate discrimination on campus, Harvard's recent failure to create a safe and non-discriminatory environment for Jewish students threatens the University's funding for research, scholarships, and more.

Your Historic Opportunity

You have been president of Harvard, one of the most important institutions in the world, for four months at one of the most challenging times in its history. As Harvard's leader, your words and actions are followed closely. As a result, the steps you take to address antisemitism at Harvard will be recognized around the world, and can contribute greatly as an example to other institutions seeking to eliminate antisemitism in all of its forms.

History has taught us that when the sparks and initial flames of antisemitism emerge, we must promptly put out the flames before a conflagration begins. It is therefore critically important you act with alacrity in addressing these issues. I encourage you to act boldly and promptly to eliminate this scourge at Harvard.

I also call upon you to complete the commitment you made at inauguration when you stated that "Knowledge is our purpose. We serve that purpose best when we commit to open inquiry and freedom of expression as foundational values of the academic community." Harvard must create an environment where free speech is encouraged and accepted. At the same time, the Harvard community at large must understand the difference between speech protected by the First Amendment and speech that incites violence or seeks the elimination of any group. Such speech does not advance knowledge, nor does it belong on campus regardless of whether or not it is protected by the First Amendment.

Successfully addressing antisemitism at Harvard and creating an environment with true freedom of expression will become a critically important part of your legacy as the Harvard community works together to address these challenges at a difficult time in world history.

I would be delighted to help in any way that I can to enable you to succeed in this mission and as Harvard's president. Please let me know what more I can do to help.

Sincerely,

William A. Ackman
A.B. 1988, MBA 1992

cc: The Harvard Corporation Board;
Penny Pritzker, Chairman

When Israel Must Consider the Nuclear Option[1]

Professor Alan Dershowitz is one of Israel's most prominent defenders outside the Jewish state. He has just written—in record time—a book about the events of October 7: *War Against the Jews: How to End Hamas Barbarism*. It will be published next month and will argue, among other things, that the Hamas attack "has required Israel to consider its nuclear option as a last resort to assure its survival." I spoke to Professor Dershowitz and asked him first, about another of the book's arguments, that there should be no absolute distinction between civilians and combatants in Gaza, but instead "a continuum of civilianality."

"It existed in Nazi Germany," he said. "There were the SS troops; there were soldiers drafted into the German army; people who enthusiastically went to the Nuremberg rallies and screamed 'Kill the Jews'; those who disclosed the hiding places of Jews; those who refused to help Jews. The same thing is true in Gaza. The most

---

1   Paul Wood, "Alan Dershowitz: when Israel must consider the nuclear option," *The Spectator*, November 7, 2023, https://thespectator.com/topic /alan-dershowitz-israel-nuclear-war-iran-gaza/.

civilian, obviously, are young children. The most non-civilian are the terrorists. In the middle, there's a wide range: people who allow their homes to be used to store rockets, people who helped in the coup to overthrow the Palestinian Authority, those who voted for Hamas.

"I want to emphasize that this is a conceptual framework. It's theoretical," he continued. "I'm not suggesting that this is an operational criteria, so that decisions can actually be made on the basis of this continuum, only that it exists. Every government should always err on the side of regarding somebody as on the civilian end of the continuum, unless there's evidence to the contrary."

Some time ago, I interviewed a Palestinian woman who had volunteered to be an Islamic Jihad suicide bomber, and she said she could happily kill Israeli children because they would grow up to be soldiers—that every Jew in Israel, young or old, was a settler on Palestinian land. I asked Dershowitz, aren't your arguments like hers? "The idea that a child will grow up to be a soldier is simply an absurd argument," he replied. "It would mean there are no such things as civilians. A three-year-old, in my continuum, is completely a civilian, until they grow up to be a terrorist. If he's fifteen, as a terrorist, he's an adult. If you're old enough to kill a Jew, you're old enough to be killed by a Jew. You can't hide behind being a child when Hamas uses child soldiers. They do it all the time, they do it to take advantage of Israeli law, because Israeli law does treat children below a certain age somewhat differently. . . There's a sensible continuum of civilianality, and there's a nonsensical one, the one that says every Jew is a settler."

Hamas told me it was right to kill the people at the concert in the desert because Israel is a mobilized society and there were a lot of reservists there.

"Remember that many people at the festival are peaceniks, very much opposed to Israel's policy in Gaza and in the West Bank. And they are not living in the settlements," Dershowitz pointed out. "Some are descendants of people who have lived in what was called Eretz Israel since before the birth of Mohammed. In 1840, they did the first demographic survey of Jerusalem, and the vast majority of people were Jewish. . . Reservists are a close question. There's nothing clear in the law about whether a reservist who is a civilian is a target. The answer is almost certainly no. When you have a war like this, the rules are very much in flux. Morality has a role to play."

A Palestinian official once told me that what the Holocaust meant to him was that a Polish Jew was living in his grandmother's house, in what is now Israel. People in Gaza look through the fence at land that used to belong to their parents and grandparents. Moshe Dayan, Israel's most celebrated soldier, gave a famous speech in 1956, a eulogy for a young Israeli killed at the Nahal Oz kibbutz (the site of one of the October 7 massacres). He said: "Why should we complain of their hatred for us? . . . they sit in the refugee camps of Gaza, and see, with their own eyes, how we have made a homeland of the soil and the villages where they and their forebears once dwelt."

"I know the speech. Dayan wasn't always right," Dershowitz replied. "If the Arab leaders in 1948 had accepted the UN partition, there would have been no refugee problem to speak of. It was completely the fault of the Arab leadership. The refugee problem was caused twice, in '48 and '67, both wars initiated by the Arabs, wars of destruction against the Jews. . . Hundreds of thousands of Pakistanis and Indians look across their border and say, 'You see that house, that's the house my grandmother used to live in.' In areas of the Czech Republic [Germans can say], 'This is a home that my grandparents used to live in.' Every Sephardic Jew could point to a house in Morocco or Algeria and say, 'That's where my grandparents lived, and now some Arab is living there.' So it's just three on a scale of ten. It's not a nine, it's not an eight. It's not a justification for killing."

But Dayan's point—one of them—was that the Palestinians of Gaza resent Israelis, and maybe they have reason to, I responded.

"The Palestinians have been fed resentment. I would feel resentment too if my own people didn't accept me," Dershowitz said. "Remember when this transfer of population occurred? The Jews of North Africa were welcomed to Israel, whereas the Arabs were put into refugee camps. . . Why are the refugee camps in Gaza? It's only just to breed resentment, so that people can look across the border and say, 'That was my grandmother's house.'"

So, I asked, the Palestinians have to accept what happened in '48?

"'48 didn't 'happen.' '48 was a decision made by the Arab leadership to invade Israel," Dershowitz replied. "Every time Israel was invaded, they got more land. . . Kaliningrad was a completely German town and now it is 100 percent Russian. That was the result of Germany invading Russia. When you invade people, you lose territory, and when you lose territory, you create refugees. There has to be a statute of limitations on this kind of thing: 1948? We're talking seventy-five years. Get over it! I'm not saying get over it when it comes to people dying, [just] when it comes to exchanges of population.

"And turn to your real enemies; the real enemies in Gaza are Hamas. . . Gaza could have been a beautiful place, Singapore on the Mediterranean. But instead of using the money [from international aid] to feed and educate their children, they use it to build tunnels and build rockets. It's hard to blame Israel for that."

Professor Paul Walzer, the theorist of armed conflict, says Israel should wage a war of justice, not vengeance.

"I completely disagree with those Israeli right-wingers talking about 'animals,'" Dershowitz said. "That's improper talk for anybody, certainly for anybody in the government . . . but there's no comparison to what Hamas says about Israel. Shakespeare said, in *The Merchant of Venice*, 'If you wrong us, shall we not revenge?' Revenge is an important element of human feelings. But I think the military really makes some decisions here. They're thinking about how to prevent a recurrence of this. That's the motivating, dominating consideration. If the rules are that you never hit a target if there are civilians, the United States and Great Britain would not have won World War Two. Dresden, Hiroshima, Nagasaki, Berlin, Tokyo: Roosevelt and Churchill said we will stop at nothing to win.

"Many more civilian casualties existed in the Afghan war and the Iraq war [than in Israel's wars]. Israel has had fewer civilian casualties than any country in modern history waging comparable wars.

That's a statistic that cannot be disputed. Let me give you one more statistic. The Israeli military announced that one in five rockets fired from Gaza misfires and lands there. One in five. More than a thousand. Every time somebody's killed by a Hamas rocket, it is blamed on Israel. Israel did not target the [al-Ahli] hospital. And yet that's the blood libel that's been circulating throughout the Arab press, and even in many parts of the Western world: that Israel targeted the hospital deliberately to kill civilians."

You could deliberately choose targets for bombing that stay within the letter of international law, while killing many civilians. A senior retired Israeli general said you should put pressure on the whole population of Gaza to get the hostages released. I read that the Israeli army has loosened its rules of engagement to fight in Gaza. I asked Dershowitz: how far should Israel go to win? How much blood should be shed?

"Remember, the blood that will be shed will be both Israeli and Palestinian. The hostages are in danger; Israeli soldiers are in danger. These are impossible calculations," he replied. "The one thing Israel shouldn't do is accept the phony morality of the United Nations or Amnesty International. Amnesty International's branch at Harvard blamed October 7 on Israel. So Israel should not accept the double-standard fake morality of outsiders. It should impose its own morality together with its allies, the United States and Great Britain, and come to a balanced, reasonable conclusion. Israel should never ever, under any circumstances target a civilian. That's a clear rule."

You could argue that Israel killing one civilian to take out one Hamas fighter is proportionate, but what about thirty civilians? Or 300?

"You never bomb a hospital, and that's why Hamas uses hospitals," Dershowitz responded. "You do bomb mosques, though, because mosques are used as ammunition depots. You try to avoid as many civilian deaths as possible. If it's the [military] head of Hamas, if it's the man who's planning all these bombs, the number could be thirty, forty, fifty, if not 100, if not 1,000. Proportionality merely means that if you have a legitimate military target—and getting rid of Hamas is legitimate—the value of the target must exceed the cost to the civilians. That is a balance that must be struck and struck, in the first instance, by the country making the decision. Remember too the use of human shields. If I hold up a bank and grab a hostage, and a policeman takes aim at me but accidentally kills the hostage, it's the hostage taker who's guilty of the murder. That's true in international law as well."

Dershowitz says in his new book that the Hamas attack—perhaps sponsored by Iran—means Israel will ultimately have to "consider its nuclear option."

"If Israel's very existence is seriously endangered by an Iranian nuclear arsenal, it will, as a last resort, likely act preventively or reactively with all weapons at its disposal," he told me.